United States
of America

United States of America

by Michael Burgan

Enchantment of the World™
Second Series

Children's Press®

An Imprint of Scholastic Inc.

New York Toronto London Auckland Sydney
Mexico City New Delhi Hong Kong
Danbury, Connecticut

Frontispiece: The Statue of Liberty

Consultant: David R. Smith, Academic Advisor and Adjunct Assistant Professor of History, University of Michigan–Ann Arbor

Please note: All statistics are as up-to-date as possible at the time of publication.

Book production by Herman Adler

Library of Congress Cataloging-in-Publication Data

Burgan, Michael.
 United States of America / by Michael Burgan.
   p. cm.—(Enchantment of the world. Second series)
 Includes bibliographical references and index.
 ISBN-13: 978-0-531-18488-2
 ISBN-10: 0-531-18488-9
 1. United States—Juvenile literature. I. Title.
 E178.3.B928 2008
 973—dc22   2007024016

SCHOLASTIC, CHILDREN'S PRESS, and associated logos are trademarks and/or registered trademarks of Scholastic Inc.
1 2 3 4 5 6 7 8 9 10 R 17 16 15 14 13 12 11 10 09 08

United States
of America

Contents

Cover photo:
A girl at the Golden
Gate Bridge

Mount Rainier

Bald eagle

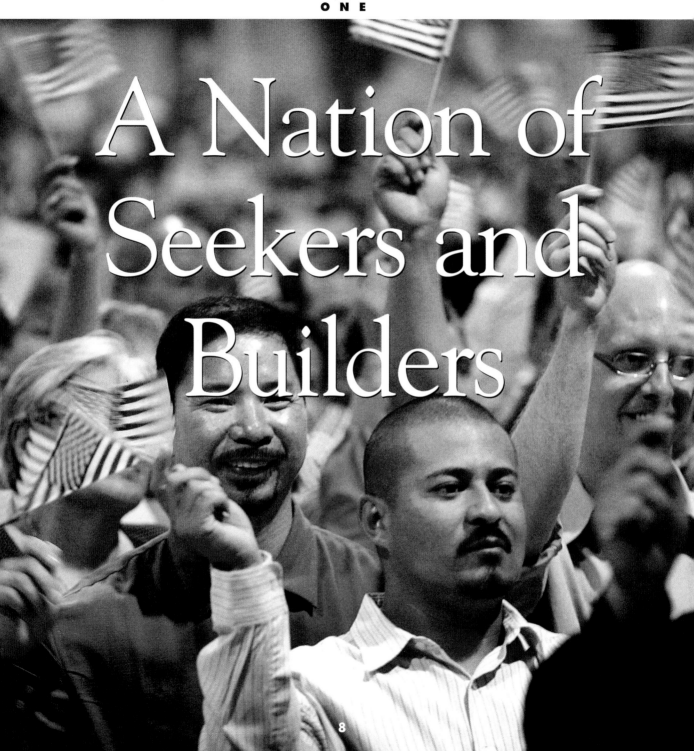

A Nation of Seekers and Builders

FOR HUNDREDS OF YEARS, PEOPLE AROUND THE GLOBE HAVE left their homelands to settle in what is now the United States of America. Leaving behind their familiar places and habits wasn't always easy. But something—the pull of a better way of life, the push of hardships at home—drove them to make that bold move. The United States has been rightly called a nation of immigrants, and each year about 1.5 million people make it their new home.

The land the newcomers settled has not always been called the United States. Settlers from Europe and enslaved people

Opposite: **Immigrants in California wave flags after being sworn in as U.S. citizens.**

An Italian family arrives at Ellis Island in New York City in 1905.

from Africa built new homes in a number of colonies with a variety of names: New Spain, Florida, New Netherland, Massachusetts. Only in 1776 did the United States of America emerge as a nation, and even then it took a long war against Great Britain to gain its independence.

Building a Nation

The founders of the United States wanted to build a prosperous nation. The country had rich land for farming and was filled with natural resources. Over the decades, the nation expanded beyond its first borders, eventually reaching from "sea to shining sea," that is to say from the Atlantic to the Pacific. Today, the American states include the cold, distant terrain of Alaska and the sunny Pacific islands of Hawai'i.

The Battle of Bennington was fought on August 6, 1777, in Vermont. It was an important American victory in the Revolutionary War.

Workers tend machinery at a textile mill in Boston, Massachusetts. Many immigrants worked in textile mills.

As the borders of the United States expanded, the nation grew wealthier. Merchants and business owners invested in banks and trade. People built factories that produced cloth, steel, household goods, and much more. Factories, mines, and farms often provided jobs for immigrants. Some of these new-comers grew rich through hard work or new ideas. With the efforts of millions of people, the United States became one of the wealthiest nations the world has ever known. But this wealth came at a price.

Hard Times Along the Way

Many people suffered to build this nation. Native Americans were killed by disease and warfare. They lost most of their land to European settlers. Africans were kidnapped from their homes and forced to become slaves in America. Even when slavery ended in 1865, African Americans endured prejudice.

The civil rights movement intensified during the 1960s. In June 1963, protesters marched in Detroit, Michigan.

They were treated poorly because of the color of their skin. The battle to create true equality for all Americans still goes on today.

Asians and Hispanics have also faced racism and unfair treatment. And being white with European roots did not guarantee an easy time. Generations of immigrants were forced to live in poor housing and take hard, low-paying jobs. Today, some U.S. workers of all backgrounds struggle to pay medical bills and send their children to college.

What Kind of Nation?

Americans often debated what kind of nation they wanted to build. Thomas Jefferson, the third U.S. president, wanted a nation of farmers. Others of his day thought the country's future was in manufacturing and trade. Today, the United States is a world leader in producing crops such wheat and corn. It is also a powerhouse in trade. Its cars, electronics, and machinery are used all over the world.

Americans have also debated what role their country should play in world affairs. In the twentieth century, the United States emerged as the strongest military power in the world. At times, it has used its strength to defend other nations and promote democracy. But it has also entered wars that some Americans did not think the country should fight. In 2003, the United States went to war with Iraq. Americans continue to argue over the wisdom of that decision.

Despite disagreements about the role of the United States in the world, the country has admirers around the globe. Young people in almost every country enjoy films and music made in the United States. From these, they learn to dress and talk as Americans do. And people hoping to build better lives still come to the United States. They seek what has been called the American Dream, the idea that through hard work, it is possible to make better lives for themselves and their children.

American soldiers wait for their flight home from Iraq.

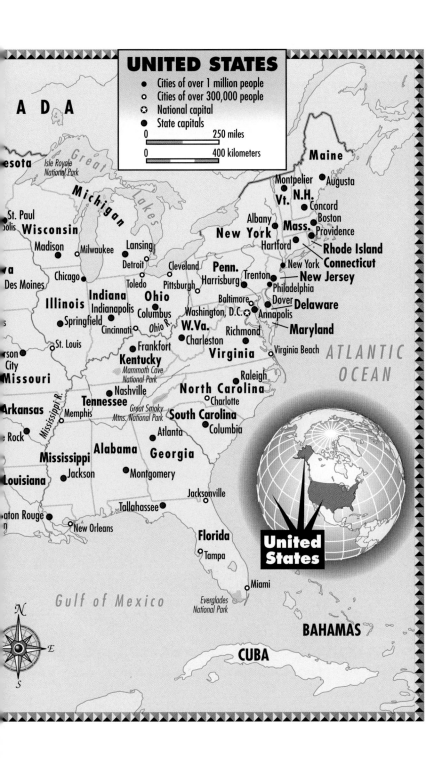

UNITED STATES

- Cities of over 1 million people
- Cities of over 300,000 people
- National capital
- State capitals

0 — 250 miles
0 — 400 kilometers

A D A

esota
Isle Royale
National Park

Great Lakes

Michigan

St. Paul
olis
Wisconsin
Madison
Milwaukee
Lansing
Detroit
Cleveland
a
Des Moines
Chicago
Toledo
Pittsburgh
Indiana
Ohio
Penn.
Harrisburg
Trenton
Illinois
Indianapolis
Columbus
Springfield
Cincinnati
Ohio R.
St. Louis
Frankfort
W.Va.
Baltimore
Dover
Delaware
Washington, D.C.
Annapolis
Kentucky
Charleston
Richmond
Maryland
Mammoth Cave
National Park
Virginia
Virginia Beach

Maine
Montpelier
Augusta
Vt.
N.H.
Concord
Albany
Boston
New York
Mass.
Providence
Hartford
Rhode Island
New York
Connecticut
New Jersey
Philadelphia

son
City
Missouri

Arkansas
e Rock

Mississippi R.
Memphis
Tennessee
Nashville
Great Smoky
Mtns. National Park
North Carolina
Charlotte
South Carolina
Columbia
Atlanta

Raleigh

ATLANTIC
OCEAN

Mississippi
Jackson
Alabama
Montgomery
Georgia

Louisiana
aton Rouge
New Orleans

Jacksonville
Tallahassee

Florida
Tampa

Miami

United
States

Gulf of Mexico

Everglades
National Park

BAHAMAS

CUBA

N
E
S

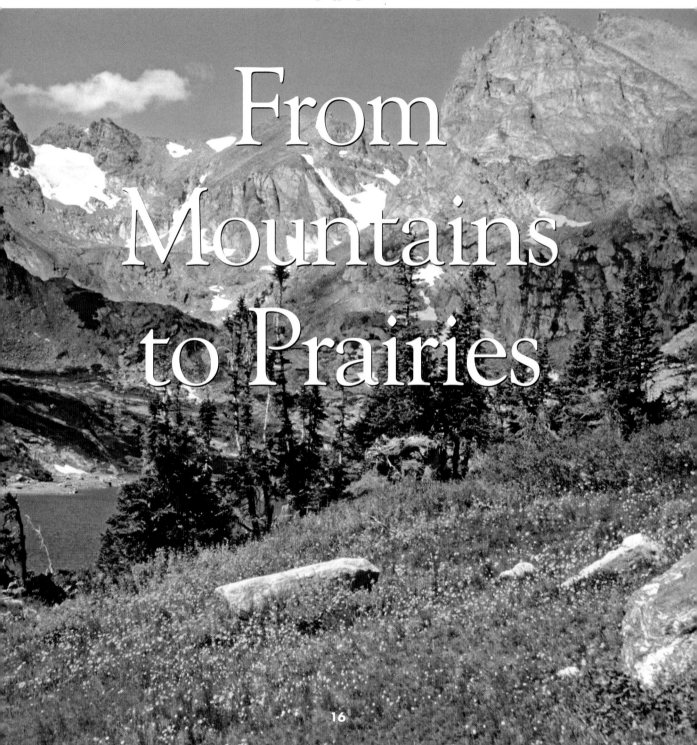

From Mountains to Prairies

The Great Plains region lies east of the Rocky Mountains and covers most of the central United States. Bison can be seen at Custer State Park in South Dakota.

THE FIRST EUROPEAN EXPLORERS OF NORTH AMERICA were amazed at the natural wonders they saw. John Smith sailed along the New England coast and found vast forests and fertile land. In Florida, Spanish explorers came upon coastal waters filled with fish. Far across the continent, Spanish settlers crossed a vast desert as they made their way into what is now New Mexico.

No one explorer or group of settlers could truly appreciate the size and diverse beauty of the land that would become the United States. Within its fifty states are towering mountain ranges; powerful, rushing rivers; and immense, flat plains.

Opposite: **Some of the highest peaks in the United States are in the Rocky Mountains.**

From Mountains to Prairies **17**

The United States' Geographic Features

Area: 3,619,969 square miles (9,375,677 sq km)

Longest Shared Border: 5,522 miles (8,887 km), with Canada

Highest Elevation: Mount McKinley, Alaska, 20,320 feet (6,194 m)

Lowest Elevation: Death Valley, California, 282 feet (86 m) below sea level

Longest River: Mississippi River, 2,340 miles (3,766 km)

Largest Lake: Lake Superior, 350 miles (563 km) long and 160 miles (257 km) wide

Highest Recorded Temperature: Death Valley, California, 134°F (57°C), July 10, 1913

Lowest Recorded Temperature: Endicott Mountains, Alaska, -80°F (-62°C), January 23, 1971

Highest Average Annual Precipitation: Mount Waialeale, Hawai'i, 460 inches (1,168 cm)

Lowest Average Annual Precipitation: Cow Creek, California, 1.6 inches (4 cm)

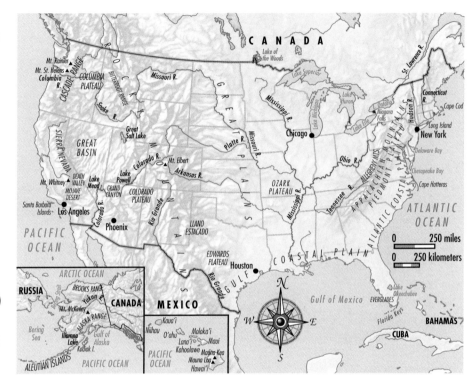

The Lay of the Land

The United States forms the center of the continent of North America. It is bordered by Canada to the north and Mexico to the south. Along the eastern coast is the Atlantic Ocean, while the Pacific Ocean lies to the west. The body of water separating Texas and Florida is called the Gulf of Mexico.

The United States is the fourth-largest country in the world in area, after Russia, Canada, and China. The forty-eight states connected to one another on the North American continent are sometimes called the continental United States or the Lower Forty-Eight.

The Eastern United States

The United States can be divided into distinct areas. Along the Atlantic Ocean are coastal plains. Near the shore, this region is generally sandy or marshy. Farther inland, it is often prime farmland. The coastal plain runs from southeastern Maine down to Florida and then curves along the Gulf of Mexico to eastern Texas.

Coastal marshes and plains along the Gulf of Mexico in Texas are protected as part of Anahuac National Wildlife Refuge.

Farther from the shore, the land rises into hills. As the hills become taller, the region is known as the Piedmont. Still farther inland are the Appalachian Mountains. This region, which has peaks that rise to nearly 6,700 feet (2,050 meters), runs from Maine to Alabama.

The White Mountains in New Hampshire are part of the Appalachian Mountains, which extend from Maine to Alabama.

Prairies, Plains, and Mountains

West of the Appalachian Mountains the land flattens into prairie. Fields of tall grass once covered this land. Beneath the grass lay some of the world's best farmland. The prairie stretches to the Mississippi River, which roughly cuts the

When Waters Rush In

Powerful storms called hurricanes sometimes roar ashore along the Atlantic or Gulf coasts, bringing destruction. On August 29, 2005, Hurricane Katrina hit, devastating coastal areas in Alabama, Mississippi, and Louisiana. The city of New Orleans, Louisiana, suffered the worst fate. Parts of New Orleans lie below sea level. Dams called levees were supposed to hold back floodwaters, but they gave way. For days, most of the city was underwater. New Orleans is still rebuilding from the worst natural disaster in U.S. history.

United States in half. On the western side of the Mississippi, a huge, flat area called the Great Plains stretches across the central United States.

The Great Plains ends at a towering mountain range. The jagged, snow-covered Rocky Mountains run from northern New Mexico through Canada and into Alaska. The tallest peak in the Rockies in the continental United States is Colorado's Mount Elbert, which measures 14,433 feet (4,399 m).

A field of sunflowers brightens the plains of North Dakota.

From Mountains to Prairies **21**

The Colorado River flows through a series of canyons in the Southwest. Canyonlands National Park is in Utah.

West to the Pacific

An imaginary line known as the Continental Divide runs along the Rockies. On the western side of this line, rivers flow westward toward the Pacific Ocean. On the eastern side, the waters flow toward the Gulf of Mexico or the Atlantic Ocean. The Colorado, one of the rivers in this region, helped produce one of the most amazing natural wonders of the world: the Grand Canyon. Its steep, colorful cliffs tower over a deep gorge.

On the western side of the Rockies is a variety of geographic features. In the Basin and Range region, the land repeatedly shifts from small mountains to flat, dry areas. Nevada lies at the heart of this region, which also extends into neighboring states. The Basin and Range region includes Death Valley, California, the hottest spot in the United States, as well as the cooling waters of Lake Mead, on the border between Arizona and Nevada. Damming the Colorado River created Lake Mead, the largest artificial lake in the country.

Approaching the Pacific Coast, several mountain ranges pop up. Ranges in this region include the Sierra Nevada of California and the Cascades, which start in California and run north through Washington. The highest peak in the Cascades is Mount Rainier in Washington, which reaches 14,410 feet (4,392 m).

Mount Rainier in Washington is a volcano. It last erupted about 150 years ago.

Beyond the Lower Forty-Eight

The largest state, Alaska, sits some 500 miles (800 kilometers) northwest of the continental United States. It shares a 1,538-mile (2,475 km) border with Canada.

Alaska's vast expanse includes forests and flat, frozen land called tundra. The northern third of the state is located in the Arctic Circle, where temperatures often plunge to −40 degrees Fahrenheit (−40 degrees Celsius). Alaska's Mount McKinley, also called Denali, is the highest spot in the United States, reaching 20,320 feet (6,194 m) above sea level. Alaska includes a string of islands called the Aleutians, which stretch out 1,700 miles (2,700 km) from the mainland—about the distance from New York City to Denver, Colorado!

Hawai'i has five active volcanoes—Loihi, Kilauea, Mauna Loa, Hualalai, and Haleakala.

A different set of islands makes up the fiftieth state. Hawai'i sits in the Pacific Ocean about 2,100 miles (3,400 km) west-southwest of California. It includes 8 main islands and more than 130 islands all together. The Hawaiian Islands were formed by volcanoes several million years ago. Hardened black lava still covers some spots, though the islands are most famous for their silky sand beaches.

Looking at American Cities

The United States has some of the liveliest cities in the world. Its largest is New York City, with about 8.2 million people. New York City is home to the Statue of Liberty, a symbol of U.S. freedom, and the Empire State Building. It is also the heart of the country's financial industry and a leading arts center. New York was once called New Amsterdam, and it served as the capital of the seventeenth-century Dutch colony of New Netherland.

Across the continent in California, Los Angeles (below) is the second-largest U.S. city. Its 3.8 million people are spread out over a huge area linked by wide highways—roads famous for long traffic delays. In 1781, settlers from Mexico, which was a Spanish colony at the time, founded Los Angeles. Famous sites in Los Angeles include the Getty Museum and Hollywood Boulevard.

In the middle of the country is the third-largest U.S. city, Chicago (above). Some 2.8 million people live in the "city that works," which was once known for its steel mills and cattle yards. Today, Chicagoans are more likely to work behind computers. Chicago's Midwest location makes it a transportation center for the nation. Popular sites there are the Sears Tower and Navy Pier. The pier, which juts far out into Lake Michigan, has rides, restaurants, and shops and offers a grand view of the city's skyline.

In East Texas, about 2.1 million people call Houston home, making it the fourth-largest city in the United States. Houston was a sleepy little town until oil was discovered in Texas in the early 1900s. Now, it's home to many oil companies. Summers in Houston are hot and humid, but people can stay cool by visiting the city's many museums or heading to the nearby waters of the Gulf of Mexico.

El Morro is a fort in San Juan, Puerto Rico. The Spanish began construction on it in 1539.

Other islands are also part of the United States. The largest of these is Puerto Rico. It lies in the Caribbean about 1,000 miles (1,600 km) southeast of Florida. Nearby are St. Croix, St. Thomas, and St. John, which together form the U.S. Virgin Islands. Almost halfway around the world from these islands, in the Pacific Ocean, are the U.S. possessions of Guam, American Samoa, and the Northern Mariana Islands.

Water, Water Almost Everywhere

The United States has some deserts, and dry spells sometimes grip the country, but for the most part, it has plenty of freshwater. The five Great Lakes—Huron, Erie, Ontario, Superior, and Michigan—lie along the U.S.-Canada border. In fact, the border runs through all of them but Lake Michigan, which lies entirely in the United States. Ships ply the lakes, heading to the ports that dot their banks. They are also a popular spot for recreation. Other notable lakes in the United States include the Great Salt Lake of Utah, Lake Iliamna in Alaska, and Florida's Lake Okeechobee.

Niagara Falls forms part of the border between New York State and Ontario, a province in Canada.

The Mississippi River and the smaller waterways that flow into it make up one of the world's most impressive river systems. The Mississippi begins in Minnesota and flows south all the way to the Gulf of Mexico. Major rivers that feed it are the Missouri, the Ohio, the Arkansas, and the Tennessee. The Mississippi River system drains about 40 percent of the continental United States. In the western United States, major rivers include the Colorado, the Columbia, and the Rio Grande. Notable rivers in the East include the Hudson, the Connecticut, and the Cumberland.

The Mississippi River begins in Minnesota and flows all the way to Louisiana, where it empties into the Gulf of Mexico. It is an important shipping route.

An average of eight hundred tornadoes strike the United States every year. This one hit Kansas in 2004.

All Sorts of Weather

Folks in New England like to say that if you don't like the weather, wait a few minutes, and it will change! The United States experiences almost every type of weather. The overall climate is temperate—warm summers and cool winters, with few long stretches of drought or heavy rain or snow. But Hawai'i is tropical, with warm weather and heavy rain year-round. Northern Alaska has arctic conditions. Little rain or snow falls, and temperatures range from cool to freezing cold. Parts of the Southwest and the Far West are hot and dry most times of the year.

Parts of the Great Plains and the Midwest sit in a region nicknamed Tornado Alley. Tornado Alley sees more severe tornadoes than any other part of the world. In 2007, a tornado almost completely destroyed the town of Greensburg, Kansas. The twister was more than 1 mile (1.6 km) wide with winds that reached 205 miles per hour (330 kph).

Life in
the Wild

I N ILLINOIS, A GROUP OF SCHOOLCHILDREN SIFTS THROUGH the prairie soil of their state. Using picks and shovels, they hope to find bones of giant mastodons—shaggy members of the elephant family that roamed much of the United States more than ten thousand years ago. Mastodon teeth, each one weighing up to 5 pounds (2.3 kilograms), have already been uncovered where the children dig.

Though mastodons are extinct, the land they inhabited still has a wide range of wildlife. Almost two thousand different kinds of mammals, reptiles, amphibians, and birds live in the United States. Many thousands more species of insects, marine life, and plants are also found there.

Opposite: **A moose grazes in Denali National Park in Alaska.**

A boy displays a mammoth bone found in Toledo, Washington. Long ago, mammoths and mastodons roamed the United States.

Animals of the Land

With its wide range of landscapes, the United States has a huge variety of animals. In forests, mammals range from tiny chipmunks to ferocious grizzly bears. Far to the north, in Alaska's Arctic Circle, polar bears hunt for fish in cold waters. The largest bears in the world, adult male polar bears can grow more than 8 feet (2.4 m) long and weigh more than 1,500 pounds (680 kg).

In the Rocky Mountains, bighorn sheep make their way over rugged terrain. Other mountain dwellers include white-tailed deer, coyotes, and wild cats called lynx.

Between four thousand and six thousand polar bears live in Alaska.

The Great Plains was once home to huge herds of bison. For Native Americans of the plains, the bison was nature's greatest resource. The Indians ate bison meat and turned the animal's tail into brushes. Bison hides became clothes, and the bones became knives, tools, and dice. During the nineteenth century, white settlers almost killed off the mighty beast. Today, bison can again be found on the plains, though they all live on preserves or ranches.

Bison live in parks and ranches in the Great Plains region. After being hunted to near extinction, they are now protected as an endangered species.

No Horsing Around

Tens of thousands of years ago, an ancestor of the modern horse roamed what is now the United States. That animal died off, and horses did not return to North America until the Spanish brought some in 1519. Over the next few centuries, horses became an important form of transportation for both Native Americans and white settlers. Today, most horses in the United States are tame, but some wild ones can still be found on Assateague Island on the Virginia-Maryland state line and in several western states.

The desert can be a harsh home for wildlife, but some hardy animals have found a way to survive in the hot, arid landscape. Well-known desert dwellers are the rattlesnake and the Gila monster, a large lizard. Most desert creatures sleep during the hot day and then come out at night to find food.

The western diamondback rattlesnake can grow to more than 7 feet (2 m) long. This venomous snake feeds primarily on small mammals.

Water Wonders

The waters off the U.S. coasts teem with marine life. The blue whale is the largest mammal in the world—and the largest animal ever to live on Earth. A blue whale can weigh up to 150 tons (136 metric tons) and stretch 80 feet (25 m) long. That's as long as two school buses placed end to end! Sea lions live along the Pacific coast, while the smaller harbor seal lives in both oceans.

Starfish and shellfish are common along beaches. Lobsters live in cooler ocean waters and are a popular dinner in New England. Fish such as bass, trout, and salmon live in the rivers and lakes of the United States. Salmon are famous for their yearly journeys up rushing rivers to spawn, or produce baby salmon.

About two thousand blue whales live off the California coast. During the winter, they migrate south to warmer waters off Mexico and Central America.

The peregrine falcon has one of the longest migrations of any North American bird. Falcons that nest in Alaska may winter in South America.

In the Air up There

High above the forests, plains, and mountains of the United States soar hundreds of kinds of birds. They range from the tiny hummingbird, barely bigger than a person's finger, to the California condor, which has a wingspan that can reach 9 feet (2.7 m). Some of the more common American birds are the robin, owl, chickadee, and starling. The world's fastest bird, the peregrine falcon, can also be found in parts of the United States. When diving for prey, a peregrine can hit speeds of 200 miles per hour (320 kph).

The most common waterfowl in the United States are ducks and geese. Related to these webbed waterbirds are the larger swans and cranes. The trumpeter swan, found mostly in Alaska and the northern Rocky Mountain states, has a wingspan of up to 7 feet (2 m).

Pride of the Nation

In 1782, U.S. leaders debated which bird should serve as a symbol for the new nation. Patriot Benjamin Franklin argued for the turkey, saying that they were courageous. But the bald eagle won out. Eagles have long stood for power and bravery. Bald eagles live in almost every state. They're not really bald—the name comes from the white feathers on their head. The bald eagle once faced extinction, but today its numbers are on the rise. The United States is home to about sixty-five thousand bald eagles, fifty thousand of them in Alaska.

A Record-Setting Tree

In California's Sequoia National Park stands a sequoia called General Sherman. It's named for William Tecumseh Sherman, a Union general during the Civil War. General Sherman is the largest tree in the world in terms of the volume of its trunk. Its base is 36.5 feet (11.1 m) wide, and its biggest branch is wider than most cars!

Fantastic Plants

Across the United States, plant life is abundant and varied. Texans are proud of their state flower, the bluebonnet. Northern California and Oregon are famous for their giant redwood trees. These trees grow to be about 275 feet (85 m) tall. They're related to another giant tree found in California, the sequoia.

The prickly pear cactus is found throughout the Southwest. Its fruits and paddles can be eaten.

Like animals, plants have adapted to cope with desert conditions. Cactuses and other desert plants have roots that stay close to the surface, so they can easily absorb water. Warmer areas that receive more rain, such as Hawai'i, southern California, and Florida, have palm trees and colorful tropical flowers. And in the damp swamps of the South, majestic cypress trees grow.

Dangers and Protection

Americans enjoy the natural beauty of their country, but at times human activity threatens wildlife. Since the 1600s,

The Mighty Oak

No tree suggests strength like the oak. It's the most common hardwood tree found in the temperate climates of North America. More than sixty types of oak live in the United States, and in 2004 the oak became the country's national tree. One famous oak tree in U.S. history is the Charter Oak of Connecticut. Legend has it that in 1687, Connecticut's colonial charter, an important legal document, was hidden inside a huge oak so English officials could not take it—and the colony's right to rule itself.

Americans have been cutting down forests to make way for farmland and cities. At times, the spread of people into new areas has forced birds and animals from their usual homes, making it hard for them to live. In the nineteenth century, companies began building factories that often polluted the water and air.

By the twentieth century, Americans saw how human activity can endanger the environment. The U.S. government began working to protect animals threatened with extinction. In 1903, President Theodore Roosevelt set up the first national wildlife refuges. Mining, logging, and building are not allowed in the refuges, making it easier for animals to survive. In 1970, the U.S. government created the Environmental Protection Agency (EPA) to reduce pollution and further protect wildlife. Three years later, Congress passed the Endangered Species Act, which provides extra protection to animals and plants in danger of dying off completely. In 2007, some one thousand species in the United States were on the endangered species list, including the Florida panther, the California condor, the whooping crane, and the star cactus. Thanks to government protection, other species such as the American crocodile have rebounded and no longer need extra protection.

The Florida panther is one of the most endangered animals on Earth. It once roamed much of the southeastern United States, but is now limited to the southern tip of Florida.

Forging a Nation

L ONG AGO, DURING THE LAST ICE AGE, SO MUCH WATER was frozen into ice that sea levels were lower. Land peeked above the water in the narrow Bering Strait between what are now Alaska and Russia. This allowed hunters from northeastern Asia to walk to North America. They slowly spread out across the continent. Bones and tools found at a site in Virginia suggest that humans were living there as long as sixteen thousand years ago.

Opposite: **After the last ice age, people in North America hunted animals such as mammoths and mastodons with spears.**

The First Americans

The early Asian migrants were the ancestors of today's Native Americans. They tracked and killed mastodons and other

The first people in North America hunted to survive.

large game, and they added to their diet by gathering wild nuts, roots, and berries. By 1500 B.C., people in the Southwest grew corn. Soon, they were also planting beans and squash.

Native Americans who farmed began to settle down. Some built large towns. Around A.D. 800, the Anasazi settled in the Southwest. They used stone and mud bricks to erect buildings with hundreds of rooms. East of the Mississippi River, various peoples built huge earthen mounds where

they buried their dead. The most successful of these "mound builders" were the Mississippians. By about 1150, their city of Cahokia, in present-day Illinois, was home to as many as twenty thousand people.

The Spanish Arrive

In 1492, life for the native peoples of North and South America changed forever. That year, Christopher Columbus, an Italian sea captain working for Spain, guided three ships into the waters of the Caribbean. Columbus thought he had found a new sea route to Asia. He called the people he met there Indians because he thought he had reached the East Indies, a part of Asia.

Spain, like other European powers of the day, hoped to find gold, silver, and other riches in distant lands. In 1513, the

Cliff and Canyon Dwellers

The Anasazi disappeared sometime around 1350. No one knows exactly why. But they left behind some remarkable remnants of great building skills. In northern New Mexico, they built a series of villages in Chaco Canyon. One of these villages, Pueblo Bonito (right), has almost seven hundred rooms. In southern Colorado at Mesa Verde, the Anasazi built what are called cliff dwellings, homes set underneath overhanging cliffs.

Spanish explorer Juan Ponce de Léon came ashore on what he thought was a large island. Actually, he and his men had reached Florida, and they claimed it for Spain. The native tribes of the region, the Calusa and the Tequesta, chased them off.

In the decades that followed, other Spanish explorers came to what is now the southern United States looking for riches. Some Spaniards tried to force the Indians into slavery, so the Indians fought back. This was the beginning of several hundred years of warfare between Europeans and Native Americans.

St. Augustine, Florida, was one of the first European cities in North America. It was founded by Spanish settlers in 1565.

Before the Spanish

Despite his fame, Christopher Columbus was not the first European explorer to reach the Americas. That claim goes to Leif Eriksson, a Norse sailor. The Norse came from Norway and settled in Iceland and Greenland. Around A.D. 1000, Eriksson led an expedition that came ashore in Newfoundland, Canada. Eriksson called the land he found Vinland. Hostile native peoples and the long distance from Iceland probably led the Norse to give up their Vinland colony. All that remains are some iron nails and building sites.

The First African Americans

In 1526, the Spanish tried to start a colony in what is now South Carolina. The effort failed, but the expedition marks the first time enslaved Africans reached what is now the United States. After the Spanish abandoned the colony, a few of the slaves remained behind and lived with the Indian tribes of the region.

English colonists settled at Roanoke Island in 1587. When the leader of the colony returned after being away for three years, all of the colonists had mysteriously disappeared.

The Spanish tried to start colonies in North America. Their priests founded missions, where they taught their Roman Catholic beliefs to the Indians. Soldiers built forts to help defend the settlers during wartime. The first permanent European settlement in the United States was the Spanish town of St. Augustine, Florida. It was founded in 1565. In 1598, Juan de Oñate led settlers from Mexico into New Mexico and founded a colony, which after 1607 was centered around Santa Fe.

European Rivals

France and England also sent explorers across the ocean. In what would become Canada, the French set up trading posts and missions. French traders traveled around the Great Lakes and sometimes ventured into what became U.S. lands. In 1585, the English tried to start a colony on Roanoke Island, off North Carolina, but it failed.

In the seventeenth century, the English had better luck founding colonies. In 1607, about one hundred settlers landed in Jamestown, Virginia. They struggled to stay alive, fighting disease and starvation. At times, they also battled the Powhatan Indians. But the Jamestown settlement survived, making it the first permanent English settlement in North America.

Farther north, in Massachusetts, English settlers now known as the Pilgrims reached Plymouth in 1620. Some of the Pilgrims were devout Christians known as Separatists. They believed that England's national church did not follow the teachings of the Bible. In Plymouth, the Separatists hoped to create a society based on their strict religious views, far from the watchful eye of English officials.

A Helping Hand

Wherever Europeans settled, they needed the help of Native Americans to survive. The local tribes provided them with food and taught them how to grow local crops. One of the most important of these Native American helpers was Tisquantum, who was also called Squanto. A member of the Wampanoag tribe, Tisquantum had been kidnapped by an English sailor and sold as a slave in Spain. He managed to escape and fled to England, where he learned to speak English. Tisquantum then made his way home to Massachusetts. He served as a translator for the Pilgrims and taught them where to fish and how to plant corn.

Other countries also laid claim to parts of North America. In 1624, Dutch settlers began to reach New Netherland, land the Netherlands claimed along the Hudson River. Sweden founded New Sweden farther south, along the Delaware River, in 1638.

Through the seventeenth century, England sent more settlers to what became the United States than any other nation. Puritans, like the Separatists of Plymouth, wanted the freedom to worship as they chose. They founded the colony of Massachusetts Bay. Roman Catholics went to Maryland, where they hoped to escape English laws that limited the rights of Catholics. Other colonists were fleeing poverty in Europe.

The Rise of Slavery

Not all immigrants to America came because they wanted to. Tens of thousands of Africans were captured in their homelands and forced into slavery. The slave trade between Africa and North America grew slowly during the 1600s but then exploded in the early 1700s. In 1650, about 1,600 people of African descent lived in British North America. By 1750, that number had risen to 236,420, about one-fifth of the total population.

Enslaved Africans were used to work on plantations that grew such crops as tobacco, rice, sugar, and indigo. In England's colonies, most slaves lived in the South, where large plantations were more common, but every colony had some slaves.

Great Britain Takes Control

By the early eighteenth century, Great Britain had a string of colonies along the Atlantic coast from Maine to the Carolinas.

It had taken control of New Netherland and New Sweden. But Spain still had colonies in Florida and New Mexico. In 1769, the Spanish sent an expedition into California, and Father Junípero Serra founded a mission in San Diego. Twenty more Spanish missions would follow in California. France also had influence. French trappers and traders set up trading posts along the Mississippi River, and the French founded New Orleans in 1718.

The interests of the European powers often clashed. The French and the British competed to control the fur trade with the Indians around the Great Lakes and along the Ohio River. This led to wars. The biggest of these wars began in 1754 and is known in the United States as the French and Indian War. By the war's end in 1763, France had lost its lands east of the Mississippi.

The Battle on Snowshoes was fought during the French and Indian War. British troops vied with the French for control of Upstate New York.

Winning the French and Indian War in the colonies had been costly for Great Britain. Its king, George III, decided that the American colonies should pay higher taxes to help pay for the cost of military defense.

In 1764, the British Parliament passed the Sugar Act. It raised or added new taxes on certain goods brought into the colonies. The next year, Parliament passed the Stamp Act, requiring that Americans pay a tax any time they bought printed materials, such as books, newspapers, legal documents, or even playing cards. Many Americans protested these taxes. They believed their rights as English citizens were being denied. Because they did not elect members of Parliament, the colonists had no say in the debate over the taxes. "Taxation without representation is tyranny!" became the popular cry.

The Boston Massacre was an important event leading to the American Revolution. British troops killed five colonists in a clash on the streets of Boston.

Protests in Boston and other colonial cities led Parliament to repeal the Stamp Act. But other taxes soon followed, and by 1768, British troops were stationed in Boston to keep order. In 1770, British soldiers fired on a crowd, killing five colonists in what became known as the Boston Massacre.

In 1773, Bostonians protested a tax on tea by throwing 342 crates of tea leaves into Boston Harbor. The British responded by sending even more troops to Massachusetts. Then, in April 1775, British and Massachusetts troops clashed in the towns of Lexington and Concord. Patriot leaders decided to go to war against the British. The American Revolution had begun.

American colonists dressed as Native Americans dumped chests of tea in Boston Harbor in what is known as the Boston Tea Party. The British responded by closing down the harbor.

Independence

At first, the colonists hoped they could settle their disagreements with King George. But soon, Patriot leaders decided that winning independence was the only way to protect their freedom. On July 4, 1776, they issued the Declaration of Independence. Its main author, Thomas Jefferson, wrote that Americans were seeking to defend their right to "life, liberty, and the pursuit of happiness."

With French help, the Americans defeated the British in 1783. The thirteen colonies were now the United States of America.

Divided Loyalties

Not all Americans supported the American Revolution. The second U.S. president, John Adams, suggested that as many as one-third of Americans remained loyal to Great Britain. Many of these Loyalists eventually fled north to what is now Canada. Another third of Americans did not actively support either side.

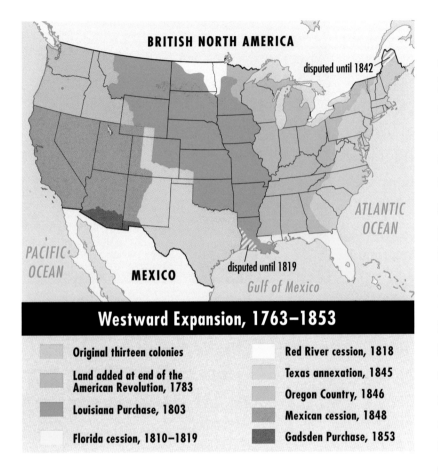

BRITISH NORTH AMERICA

disputed until 1842

ATLANTIC OCEAN

PACIFIC OCEAN

MEXICO

disputed until 1819

Gulf of Mexico

Westward Expansion, 1763–1853

- Original thirteen colonies
- Land added at end of the American Revolution, 1783
- Louisiana Purchase, 1803
- Florida cession, 1810–1819
- Red River cession, 1818
- Texas annexation, 1845
- Oregon Country, 1846
- Mexican cession, 1848
- Gadsden Purchase, 1853

Running the new country was not easy. Initially, the government was based on a document called the Articles of Confederation. Under the articles, the national government had few powers and could not force the states to pay taxes or follow laws. In 1787, leaders met to improve the Articles of Confederation. In the end, they created a whole new government based on a document called the Constitution. It balanced power between the states and the national government. In 1789, George Washington was elected the first president under the Constitution.

Growing Pains

It wasn't long before the United States went to war with Great Britain once again. The War of 1812 was largely fought to defend the United States' right to trade as it wished. When a peace treaty was signed in 1815, the young country had shown the world it would fight to protect its interests.

During the early nineteenth century, the first factories appeared in New England. Textile companies hired women and children to turn cotton and wool into cloth. Because of this growing demand, cotton was becoming the main crop in the South. As plantation owners increased cotton production, slavery grew. By the 1830s, slavery was illegal or on the way out in the Northern states. Some Northerners wanted to abolish, or end, slavery all across the country, but Southern plantation owners believed they could not survive without it. In Congress, lawmakers often debated whether to limit the spread of slavery in new territories.

The Louisiana Purchase

In 1803, the size of the United States doubled when the country bought the Louisiana Territory from France. The Louisiana Purchase included lands from the Mississippi River to the Rocky Mountains and from the Gulf Coast to Canada. To explore these new lands, President Thomas Jefferson sent Meriwether Lewis and William Clark on an expedition. The explorers made their way across the continent all the way to the Pacific Ocean. Their efforts opened the Far West to trade and settlement.

That issue had greater importance after 1848. Two years before, President James Polk had launched a war against Mexico. Polk believed in Manifest Destiny—the idea that the United States had a God-given right to control all of North America. With the U.S. victory in the Mexican War, the country acquired California and other southwestern lands. Southerners wanted to bring their slaves to these new lands, while Northerners tended to oppose the spread of slavery. California became the thirty-first state in 1850, and slavery was not allowed there. But in other former Mexican lands, settlers were allowed to decide for themselves whether to allow slavery.

Union soldiers prepare for battle against the Confederate armies in Arlington, Virginia, in August 1865.

The Civil War

In 1860, Abraham Lincoln won the presidency. He wanted to prevent the spread of slavery in new U.S. territories and states, but he promised not to end slavery where it already existed. Southerners did not believe Lincoln. By April 1861, eleven Southern states had seceded, or broken away, from the Union, and formed a new country called the Confederate States of America. Lincoln said it was illegal for the states to secede, and that he would not allow it. This was the beginning of the Civil War.

Leading Others to Freedom

During the years of slavery in the United States, thousands of African Americans who were held in slavery ran away from their masters. One was Harriet Tubman. In 1849, Tubman escaped from her slave masters in Maryland. She then risked her freedom—and her life—by returning to the South several times to help other slaves escape. During the Civil War, she served as a nurse, spy, and military scout for the Union. After the war, Tubman traveled the country giving speeches about her experiences and fought for the legal rights of African Americans who had been freed from slavery.

From 1861 to 1865, more than six hundred thousand Americans died as the North battled the South. In the end, the North won. This meant the end of slavery in the United States. The years following the war were called Reconstruction, as the North helped the Southern states rebuild after the war. The winners also tried to create new governments in the

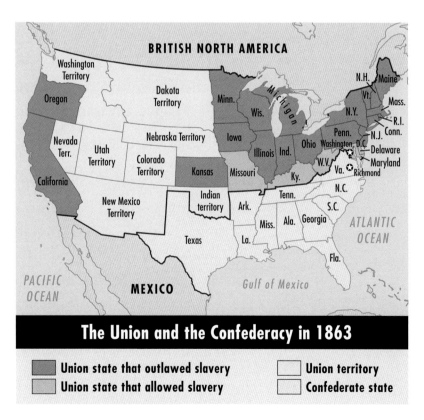

The Union and the Confederacy in 1863

- Union state that outlawed slavery
- Union state that allowed slavery
- Union territory
- Confederate state

Seeing the Light

One of the world's greatest inventors was Thomas Edison, who was born in 1847. His work as a telegraph operator prompted Edison to study electricity and sound. In 1877, he invented the first device for recording and playing back sounds—the phonograph. He also perfected the incandescent bulb, the lighting still used in most homes today. Edison created a company to bring electricity to homes and businesses so they could use his bulbs and other products later developed to run on electricity. Edison also developed a movie camera and projector, helping to create the motion picture industry in the United States. During his life, Edison held more than a thousand patents, legal documents acknowledging a new invention. He died in 1931.

South that would help protect the rights of the former slaves. For the most part, though, white Southerners resisted the effort to give African Americans their legal rights, such as voting.

Industrial Giant

By this time, the U.S. economy was changing. Workers left farms to take jobs in factories. Items once made by hand were now made by machines. This shift to using machines on a large scale is called the Industrial Revolution.

The new industrial economy used vast natural resources. Coal was dug from the ground and used to power steam engines. Iron ore was turned into steel. In the 1870s, Andrew Carnegie, a Scottish immigrant, founded what grew into the world's largest steel company.

In the mid-nineteenth century, immigrants began pouring into the country to find jobs working in mines and mills and building railroads. At the time, the largest number of immigrants came from northern Europe. A devastating famine led 1.6 million Irish to move to the United States between 1841 and 1860. After 1880, more people emigrated from southern, central, and eastern Europe, particularly Italy, Poland, and Russia. Like the immigrants before them, they took almost any job they could find, and they often faced prejudice. But most immigrants found life in the United States was better than in their former homelands.

Many immigrants made their homes on the Lower East Side of Manhattan in New York City during the late nineteenth century.

To move goods and people across the country, the United States built a railroad system unmatched in the world. As travel improved, more people headed to the Great Plains and the Far West.

This led to many changes for the Indian tribes of the West. White hunters killed off almost all the bison, and the growth of towns led to conflicts between the U.S. Army and the tribes. A series of wars was fought across the Great Plains and the Southwest. The Indians had some victories. In 1876, Sioux and Cheyenne forces defeated General George Custer at Little Bighorn, in Montana. But, the U.S. Army had more troops and better weapons. In the end, almost all the tribes were forced to live on reservations, land set aside for them by the U.S. government.

General George Armstrong Custer's U.S. cavalry troops were defeated by Sioux and Cheyenne forces at the Battle of the Little Bighorn in 1876.

American troops fought in the trenches during World War I. More than one hundred thousand American soldiers died in the war.

Becoming a World Power

By the 1890s, the U.S. economy was increasingly tied to other parts of the world. U.S. companies sold their goods overseas and bought natural resources from other countries. The desire to protect U.S. foreign interests brought the country into several wars. In 1898, the United States defeated Spain, which still controlled colonies in the West Indies and the Pacific Ocean. With this victory, the United States took control of the Philippines (a group of islands in the Pacific) and Puerto Rico.

In 1914, World War I broke out in Europe. Most Americans wanted to stay out of this conflict. U.S. leaders, however, sided with Great Britain and its allies against Germany. Eventually, after German submarines began attacking U.S. ships, the United States entered the war. Between April 1917 and November 1918, about two million U.S. troops served overseas. At home, women took jobs formerly filled by men. The war helped fuel popular support to give all American women the right to vote.

The Fight for Rights

Starting in the 1840s, some women in the United States demanded the right to vote, which is called suffrage. Susan B. Anthony, who was born in 1820, was a leader of the movement. She helped form the National Woman Suffrage Association in 1869. Anthony also wrote the first proposed amendment, or change, to the Constitution that would give women the right to vote. Anthony saw several western states grant their female residents the right to vote. But she died in 1906, before the Nineteenth Amendment passed in 1920, giving all American women the right to vote. Anthony was the first woman to appear on the front of a U.S. coin. Her picture was on a dollar coin first issued in 1979.

Boom and Bust

In the 1920s, times seemed good. The economy was improving. People enjoyed watching new sports heroes, such as baseball star Babe Ruth and boxer Jack Dempsey. Radios appeared for the first time, and films were about to add sound to their moving pictures. People began buying cars, such as Henry Ford's Model T.

People call this period the Roaring Twenties, but the good times had a dark side. Farmers were struggling as prices for their crops fell. Factories produced more goods than people could

Prohibition

During the 1920s, Americans could not legally buy alcohol. The Eighteenth Amendment to the Constitution, which passed in 1919, had created what is called Prohibition. It made the production and sale of alcohol a crime. But alcohol did not disappear. Thousands of bootleggers made or imported alcohol illegally. Much of the liquor was sold in secret bars called speakeasies. Bootleggers made a ton of money selling illegal alcohol, and violence rose as gangsters fought to control the business. The rise in organized crime, and the notion that the U.S. government should not restrict alcohol sales, led to the end of Prohibition in 1933.

afford to buy. And on "Black Thursday"—October 24, 1929—the price of many stocks plummeted. Stock prices continued to slide for several weeks. The sudden plunge in prices led to the worst economic crisis in U.S. history, the Great Depression.

By 1932, nearly one-quarter of the American workforce did not have jobs. Millions of people struggled to find food, and many people lost their life savings when banks suddenly went out of business. In 1933, Franklin D. Roosevelt was elected president. Over the next six years, Roosevelt created a number of programs that came to be called the New Deal. The government paid workers to build bridges, roads, and airports. It created Social Security to give money to the elderly, the disabled, and people without jobs. The New Deal programs did not end the Great Depression. But they did help millions of people and gave them hope for better days.

During the Depression, millions of people had no money to buy food. Here, unemployed men line up to receive a free meal.

World War Again

Before better days arrived, though, the United States had to go through another world war. World War II officially began in 1939, when Germany invaded Poland. Great Britain and France united to help the Poles, but Germany soon took over much of Europe. In 1941, the Soviet Union, a large country made up of Russia and other now-independent European and Asian nations, joined the fight against Germany. Meanwhile, war also raged in Asia as Japan tried to expand its territory. With the memory of World War I fresh in their minds, many Americans wanted to stay out of the war. But on December 7, 1941, Japan launched an attack on the U.S. naval base at Pearl Harbor, Hawai'i. Within days, the United States was at war.

A small boat rescues seamen from the USS *West Virginia*, which was damaged during the Japanese attack on Pearl Harbor in 1941.

Seeking Equality in the Air

Though black Americans fought courageously during World War II, they were not treated well. Both in and out of the military, they faced prejudice. The military, like many parts of American society, was segregated. Blacks and whites were kept separate. African American soldiers were not allowed to fight next to white Americans, and they were often given only support jobs. But a group of black flyers trained at Alabama's Tuskegee Institute proved that African Americans had the skills to serve well in the military. The Tuskegee Airmen shot down about three hundred enemy planes over Europe and won dozens of medals for their bravery. Their efforts played a part in ending segregation in the military in 1948.

By this time, the United States was the most advanced industrial nation in the world. It needed all its resources and workers to fight the war. The government ordered tens of thousands of warplanes, ships, and tanks. U.S. factories also turned out guns and supplies for the troops. This government military spending helped pull the country out of the Great Depression. The war effort provided high-paying jobs to women, African Americans, and Hispanics. Japanese Americans, however, saw their rights taken away. About 120,000 Japanese Americans, including U.S. citizens, were sent to interment camps because some U.S. leaders feared they would try to help Japan. Some Japanese American men proved their loyalty by joining the U.S. military and fighting bravely during the war.

Gradually, Germany was weakening as it fought the Soviet Union in the east. Then, on June 6, 1944, 150,000 American, British, and other western troops came ashore at Normandy, France. Within a year, Germany was defeated. In August 1945, U.S. planes dropped two atomic bombs, the most powerful weapons ever made at that time, on the Japanese cities of Hiroshima and Nagasaki. Tens of thousands of people were killed, and Japan soon surrendered.

Nearly 70 percent of the buildings in Hiroshima, Japan, were destroyed in the nuclear blast on August 6, 1945.

Postwar Challenges

At the end of World War II, the United States was the strongest, richest country in the world. Returning soldiers used money loaned from the government to buy homes. Many of these homes were in suburbs that sprang up outside major cities. The veterans also went to college in record numbers. Soon, many were making more money than their parents ever had.

Still, the country faced problems. The United States and the Soviet Union, which was a communist country, had become enemies. Communism is a system in which the government controls the economy and owns most of the businesses. The United States and the Soviet Union became locked in what was called the cold war. They did not fight each other directly but instead supported nations and groups that battled each other.

The cold war brought U.S. troops into battle in Korea, from 1950 to 1953, and in Vietnam. U.S. military advisers began working in Vietnam in the 1950s, and American combat troops arrived there in 1965. The last U.S. troops did not leave the region until 1975. By that time, more than fifty-eight thousand Americans and between two and three million Vietnamese had lost their lives in the conflict.

In 1965, civil rights marchers walked from Selma to Montgomery, Alabama. The march was led by Martin Luther King Jr. (center) and other important civil rights leaders, including John Lewis, Jesse Douglas, James Forman, and Ralph Abernathy.

The Fight for Civil Rights

Americans protested the unfair treatment many U.S. citizens received. During the 1950s, African Americans began to speak out against segregation and local laws that kept them from voting. Martin Luther King Jr. became the most famous leader in the civil rights movement. King and other civil rights leaders used nonviolent protest to bring about change. This began an era of social protest that would carry on through the 1960s, as hundreds of thousands of Americans took to the streets to protest the Vietnam War.

The protests and demands for equality upset some Americans who wanted a return to what they saw as the better times of the past. Ronald Reagan, a former governor of California, became the leader of this conservative movement. He was elected president in 1980, promising to lower taxes, reduce the size of government, and strengthen the military.

During the 1980s, relations with the Soviet Union improved, and the cold war ended in 1991. That same year, U.S. troops fought in the Gulf War, pushing invading Iraqi troops out of Kuwait. The United States remained the greatest military and economic power in the world.

Challenge for the Twenty-first Century

The country was prosperous and powerful, but on September 11, 2001, it received a terrible shock. That day, terrorists hijacked four planes and flew two of them into the twin towers at the World Trade Center in New York. A third crashed into the Pentagon, the center of the U.S. military establishment, outside Washington, D.C. The last plane crashed in a Pennsylvania field.

President George W. Bush responded by sending troops into Afghanistan. That central Asian country had protected the leaders of al-Qa'ida, the terrorist group that had carried out the hijackings. By 2002, a government friendly to the United States ruled Afghanistan. Fighting there continues, however, and the country remains unstable.

In March 2003, President Bush sent U.S. troops to Iraq. He claimed that Iraqi leader Saddam Hussein had danger-

ous weapons that threatened the United States, a claim that proved to be incorrect. Though a few nations were willing to help the United States in the Iraq War, many were not. The United States quickly toppled Hussein, but the war dragged on. By 2008, almost 4,000 U.S troops had been killed in Iraq, as had between 100,000 and 650,000 Iraqis.

As the war continues, Americans debate how best to keep the country safe. In the meantime, they go about their daily lives, working, playing, and raising families. Though the United States has not always lived up to its ideals, Americans look back on their country's history with pride.

The terrorist attacks of September 11, 2001, were the first foreign attacks on American soil since Pearl Harbor.

CHAPTER FIVE

The People's Choice

THE ENGLISH COLONISTS BROUGHT TO AMERICA A STRONG belief in self-rule. They believed that citizens should choose government leaders to represent their interests. When writing the Constitution, leaders tried to balance the rights of the states to govern themselves with the need for a national government.

The men who wrote the Constitution in 1787 believed in the separation of powers. This means that different parts of government should make the laws, enforce the laws, and interpret the laws. The U.S. government has three distinct branches to carry out these three duties. The writers of the Constitution also believed in checks and balances. Each branch has rights and duties that help it check the powers of the other two. In this way, no one branch dominates the government.

Opposite: **The U.S. Constitution was signed in Philadelphia, Pennsylvania, on September 17, 1787.**

The Bill of Rights

In 1787, some Americans did not believe the Constitution did enough to protect individual rights. They thought it should spell out certain rights that the government could never take away. As a result, the first ten amendments to the Constitution, which are known as the Bill of Rights, were approved. These rights include freedom of speech, freedom of religion, and the right to a trial by jury.

The People's Choice **67**

Choosing a President

Unlike U.S. senators and representatives, the president of the United States is not chosen by popular vote. Instead, what matters is the vote by what is known as the Electoral College. Each state gets as many electoral votes as its combined total of senators and representatives in Congress. For example, Oregon has two senators and five representatives, so it gets seven electoral votes.

The person who gets the most votes for president in any given state generally receives all of that state's electoral votes. Because of this, the person who receives the most votes in the country as a whole sometimes does not receive the most electoral votes. This happened most recently in 2000, when Al Gore received a half a million more votes than George W. Bush but had a lower total in the Electoral College.

The Executive Branch

President George W. Bush signed the Central American Free Trade Agreement in 2005.

The executive branch is responsible for carrying out, or executing, the laws of the country. The leader of the executive branch is the president. The president is elected to a four-year term of office. A vice president is elected at the same time. To be president or vice president, a person must have been born in the United States and be at least thirty-five years old. If the president dies or cannot carry out the duties of the office, the vice president becomes president.

The president has many important duties. The president signs bills into law, appoints federal judges and other important officials, and serves as commander in chief of the military.

The executive branch also includes fifteen departments under the president's

Stars and Stripes Forever

The United States flag was created during the American Revolution. By most accounts, Francis Hopkinson of New Jersey receives credit for the design of the "Stars and Stripes." Some people claim that Betsy Ross sewed the first flag, but many historians doubt this. The original flag had thirteen alternating red and white stripes and a blue patch with thirteen white stars in the upper-left corner. Over time, one star was added to the flag for each new state joining the Union. Today's flag still has thirteen stripes, along with fifty stars.

control, each focused on a particular area such as defense, justice, and transportation. The president appoints the head of each department. Together, these advisers form the president's cabinet.

Several independent agencies are also part of the executive branch. These include the National Aeronautics and Space Administration (NASA), which runs the country's space program, and the Central Intelligence Agency (CIA), which spies on foreign enemies.

The Legislative Branch

The legislative branch makes the laws of the United States. The country has 535 lawmakers, with 435 in the U.S. House of Representatives and 100 in the U.S. Senate. Together, these two lawmaking bodies are known as the U.S. Congress. Each state elects two senators. The number of representatives

Madame Speaker

The most powerful position in the U.S. House of Representatives is that of Speaker of the House. The Speaker comes from the political party that controls the most seats. In January 2007, the Democratic Party took control of the House and elected Nancy Pelosi the first female Speaker in U.S. history. Pelosi, from California, entered the House of Representatives in 1987. As a lawmaker, she has focused on health issues and protecting the rights of women.

is based on a state's population, with every state guaranteed at least one representative. Representatives serve two-year terms, while senators serve six-year terms.

Members of Congress take the oath of office on January 4, 2007.

Congress proposes laws called bills. If both houses pass a bill, it is sent to the president, who can either sign it into law or veto (reject) it. Congress can override, or overturn, a veto if two-thirds of the members of each house choose to do so.

Besides making laws, Congress has several other duties. The Senate must approve treaties with foreign nations and important appointments made by the president. Congress has the sole power to declare war against a foreign nation. It can also remove certain government officials from office if they commit crimes, in a process called impeachment.

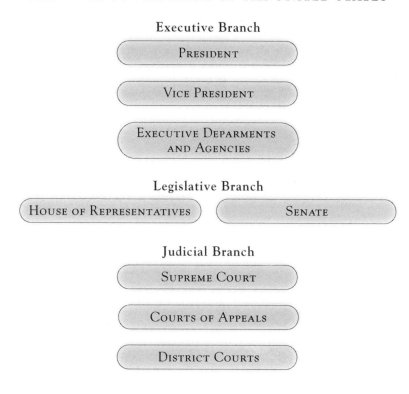

NATIONAL GOVERNMENT OF THE UNITED STATES

Executive Branch

PRESIDENT

VICE PRESIDENT

EXECUTIVE DEPARMENTS AND AGENCIES

Legislative Branch

HOUSE OF REPRESENTATIVES   SENATE

Judicial Branch

SUPREME COURT

COURTS OF APPEALS

DISTRICT COURTS

The Judicial Branch

The federal judiciary has several levels. At the lowest level are district courts. These courts hear trials involving federal laws. A decision from a district court can be appealed to a Court of Appeals. Sitting above these courts is the U.S. Supreme Court, which has one chief justice and eight

The U.S. Supreme Court building in Washington, D.C., was completed in 1935. Before that time, the Supreme Court met in the basement of the U.S. Capitol.

associate justices. Supreme Court justices, like all federal judges, are appointed for life by the president. The Supreme Court has the power to decide if a state or federal law does not follow the Constitution. A law ruled unconstitutional can no longer be enforced.

Other Levels of Government

As does the U.S. government, each state has a constitution and a bill of rights. The states also have three branches that create, enforce, and interpret state laws. All the states except Nebraska have a legislature with two houses. An elected official called a governor leads each state's executive branch. Like the U.S. president, governors can approve or veto laws. In many states, voters also elect a number of other high officials, including lieutenant governor, secretary of state, treasurer, and attorney general. Below the state government are county, city, and town governments, which are often responsible for services such as police, schools, and road maintenance.

Life of the Parties

The Constitution does not mention political parties, but they play an important role in U.S. government. Since the 1790s, the United States has had a two-party system, in which two major parties compete to control the presidency, Congress, and state and local governments. Smaller third parties usually exist, but they rarely hold much power.

Today, the two major parties are the Democratic Party and the Republican Party. Democrats tend to support using the federal government to solve such problems as poverty and pollution. Republicans usually support the interest of business. In the twenty-first century, many Americans are shedding their ties to the major parties. In 2007, about 30 percent of registered voters said they were neither Republican nor Democrat.

The National Anthem

The U.S. national anthem is called "The Star-Spangled Banner." A lawyer named Francis Scott Key wrote the words after he watched the British attack Fort McHenry in Baltimore, Maryland, during the War of 1812. The music was taken from a popular British song. The anthem was officially adopted in 1931. These are the words to the first verse.

O say, can you see, by the dawn's early light,
What so proudly we hailed at the twilight's last gleaming,
Whose broad stripes and bright stars, through the perilous fight
O'er the ramparts we watched, were so gallantly streaming?
And the rockets' red glare, the bombs bursting in air
Gave proof through the night that our flag was still there;
O say, does that star-spangled banner yet wave
O'er the land of the free and the home of the brave?

Democratic presidential nominee John Kerry (right), and his running mate, John Edwards, greet supporters at a rally before the 2004 election.

Washington, D.C.: Did You Know This?

Washington, the capital city of the United States, is located in an area called the District of Columbia. The district belongs to the federal government rather than any state. To the west of the District of Columbia lies the Potomac River, with Virginia beyond. Everywhere else, the district is bordered by Maryland. Residents of

Washington, D.C., can vote for the U.S. president. They also send one representative to the U.S. House, but this person cannot vote on bills. The district has no U.S. senators. The city government has a mayor and city council.

The District of Columbia was laid out in 1791, and it officially became the nation's capital in 1800. Important sites in Washington include the Capitol (left), where Congress meets, and the White House, where the president lives. The city also has many famous landmarks. Some honor past presidents, such as the Lincoln and Jefferson Memorials and the Washington Monument. Others honor veterans killed in World War II, Korea (above), and Vietnam. The Smithsonian Institution operates a group of museums. The city is also famous for the National Portrait Gallery and the National Zoo.

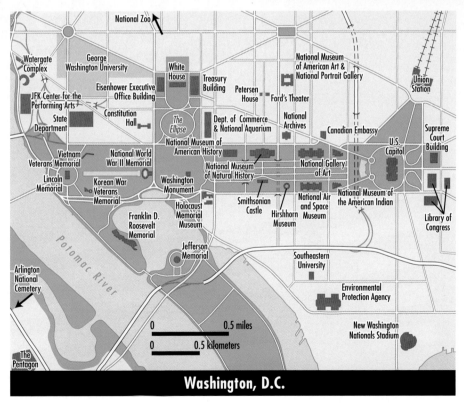

Washington, D.C.

Earning a Living

THE UNITED STATES IS THE RICHEST NATION IN THE world. Many factors have helped the United States prosper. Hardworking immigrants strive to make a better life for themselves. Businesses keep coming up with ways to improve old tools or make brand-new ones.

Today, U.S. companies come in all sizes. IBM, which is based in New York, is the world's largest computer services company, with more than three hundred thousand employees around the globe. At the same time, a growing number of Americans are working for themselves, running businesses out of their home. The mixture of businesses big and small makes the U.S. economy the most dynamic in the world.

Opposite: **IBM regional headquarters in downtown Chicago, Illinois**

Money Matters

The basic unit of money in the United States is the dollar. It is divided into 100 cents. Amounts of less than a dollar come in coins—1 cent, 5 cents, 10 cents, 25 cents, and 50 cents—better known as the penny, nickel, dime, quarter, and half-dollar. Amounts of one dollar or more are paper bills. The government has issued several dollar coins, but they have never had wide use. The fronts of both bills and coins feature historic U.S. figures such as George Washington and Thomas Jefferson. A living person may not be depicted on U.S. money. The backs often show important buildings or symbols of the nation. For example, the back of the $5 bill shows the Lincoln Memorial.

The U.S. dollar is the most popular standard of value in the world. There are more U.S. dollars in circulation worldwide than any other currency.

Down on the Farm

Native Americans and early colonists farmed to feed themselves. By the eighteenth century, Americans were producing more crops than they needed, and they sold the extra. Since then, farms have become more and more productive, so fewer people can grow more crops.

Agriculture makes up a large part of the U.S. economy today. Less than 1 percent of the country's roughly 151 million workers are involved with farming, but they produce goods worth more than US$240 billion every year. Livestock accounts just over half that total. In 2005, the country's farms raised 9 billion chickens, 96 million head of cattle, 61 million pigs, 6 million sheep, and 2.5 million goats. Iowa is the top corn-producing state, while Kansas and other Great Plains states produce the most wheat. Texas leads the nation in raising cattle, while California produces more dairy products than any other state.

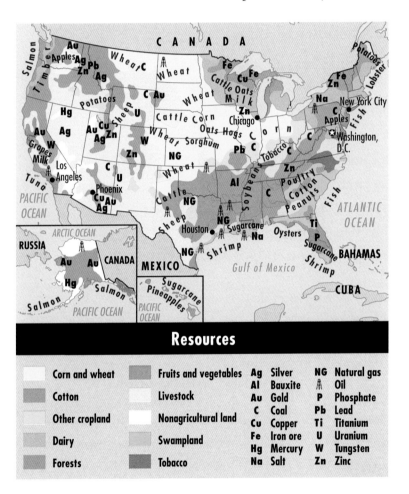

Resources

Corn and wheat	Fruits and vegetables	**Ag** Silver
Cotton	Livestock	**Al** Bauxite
Other cropland	Nonagricultural land	**Au** Gold
Dairy	Swampland	**C** Coal
Forests	Tobacco	**Cu** Copper

Fe Iron ore	**NG** Natural gas
Hg Mercury	Oil
Na Salt	**P** Phosphate
	Pb Lead
	Ti Titanium
	U Uranium
	W Tungsten
	Zn Zinc

Corn is the leading agricultural product in the United States. Much of the corn grown in the United States is used as livestock feed.

What the United States Grows, Makes, and Mines

Agriculture

Corn	10.5 million bushels
Cattle	96 million head
Milk	177 billion pounds

Manufacturing

Transportation equipment	US$653.4 billion
Food products	US$481.7 billion
Chemical products	US$447.4 billion

Mining

Oil	7.61 million barrels a day
Coal	1.05 billion metric tons
Copper	1.16 million metric tons

At a mine in Wyoming, explosives are used to break up coal. The coal is then loaded into trucks.

From Raw Materials to Finished Goods

In 2006, roughly 23 percent of U.S. workers had jobs in mining, manufacturing, or transportation. Among the most valuable natural resources is coal, which is used to create energy at power plants. West Virginia and Pennsylvania were once leading producers of coal, but now the country's largest coal mines are in Wyoming. Oil is another major source of energy, and Texas and Alaska have more of it than any other state. Other resources taken from the earth include copper, natural gas, lead, potash, clay, and stone.

Measuring Up

For weighing and measuring, the United States uses a system first brought to North America by the English. It is called the common system of measurement. The units in this system are often called customary units. Distance measurements include the inch, the foot (12 inches), the yard (3 feet), and the mile (5,280 feet). Measurements of weight include the ounce, the pound (16 ounces), and the ton (2,000 pounds). In 1988, Congress passed a law calling the metric system the preferred system of weights and measures. The metric system is based on units of 100. For example, the basic measure for distance is the meter, and 100 meters equals 1 kilometer. Despite Congress's action, few Americans except scientists and engineers use the metric system.

At the country's factories, workers make products ranging from cars and electronics to clothes and medicine. Manufacturing was once a source of well-paid jobs. In recent years, however, many U.S. companies have moved their factories overseas, where costs are cheaper. By lowering costs, they are better able to compete with foreign companies that charge lower prices for their goods. But many American factory workers have lost their jobs and have trouble finding new ones that pay well.

Some U.S. manufacturing companies have found other ways to compete. Some rely more on computerized machines. Others specialize in one item and make it better than anyone else. Boeing, for example, is one of only two major commercial airplane makers in the world. In 2006, Boeing sold 1,044 planes, worth US$114 billion.

The Car King

Henry Ford did not invent the automobile, but he made it affordable for people around the world. In 1913, Ford perfected a system called mass production. Belts and chains moved sections of his famed Model T car through his factory. Each worker did the same job over and over, attaching one piece, for example, rather than building a whole car. This cut the time it took to produce a Model T, and Ford could make more of them for less money. He then lowered the price of the car so more people could buy them. A few years later, Ford almost doubled most of his workers' salary, to US$5 a day. This meant that more of them could afford to buy the cars they helped build.

Transporting materials and goods is also big business in the United States. Trucks, trains, ships, and planes all move goods. Major airports include Chicago's O'Hare and Atlanta's Hartsfield-Jackson. The country's largest ports include the Port of South Louisiana and the Port of Houston.

The Information Revolution

During the nineteenth century, industry replaced farming as the main source of income for most Americans during a time known as the Industrial Revolution. In the twentieth century, U.S. companies helped create what has been called the Information Revolution. Workers made fewer goods and worked more with ideas. Computers helped the workers communicate with one another and work more efficiently.

Shoppers look at computers on display at an Apple store in Palo Alto, California, near the company's headquarters.

Computers first appeared during World War II, but they were as large as cars. Starting in the 1970s, several U.S. companies began creating smaller "personal" computers that could sit on a desk. Apple made the first successful personal computer in 1977, and IBM followed with its own version in 1981. Today, Apple and Dell are top U.S. personal computer makers. To work, computers need programs called software. The world's leading software maker is

Microsoft, located in Bellevue, Washington. Its cofounder, Bill Gates, is currentlyone of the world's richest persons.

The media are also a part of the Information Revolution. Traditional newspaper, radio, and television companies are increasingly providing information via the Internet. Internet companies such as Yahoo! and Google are a source for both news and entertainment.

At Your Service

Computers play a large role in what is called the service sector of the economy. This includes retail stores, banks, education, and government. The vast majority of Americans work in service industries.

Entertainment is one part of the service sector. Hollywood, California, is the center of the U.S. film industry. American

Many American companies have hired people in India to take calls from customers.

music, from rap to rock and roll, is popular around the globe. Travel and tourism is another kind of entertainment. In 2004, the travel industry had almost US$546 billion in sales.

A World Economy

U.S. workers and consumers are part of a global economy. U.S. businesses often have operations in other countries. Global concerns play a part in the decisions business leaders make.

In recent years, service-sector jobs have followed manufacturing jobs overseas. Today, U.S. companies employ computer programmers, architects, and many other skilled workers in other countries, particularly India. The United States has signed several agreements that promote trade with foreign countries.

In the North American Free Trade Agreement of 1994, the United States, Canada, and Mexico agreed to end taxes on goods traded between the three countries. In 2005, the United States signed a similar agreement with several Central American countries and the Dominican Republic, a nation in the Caribbean.

Challenges for Today and Tomorrow

The U.S. economy is always growing and changing. While it produces great wealth for some and a good living for most, millions of Americans still struggle to find jobs. Others have jobs but do not make enough money to provide for their families.

The gap in wages between the rich and the poor has been growing since the 1970s. In 2004, the wealthiest 1 percent of Americans earned three times as much as they did in 1979, but the poorest (or least wealthy) 20 percent of workers saw almost no rise in their earnings. Some Americans fear that this "wage gap" leads to great inequality in health care and education.

Health care in general is a growing concern. Starting after World War II, most workers received health insurance through their employers. This insurance helped them pay their medical bills. Since the 1990s, however, many companies have cut back on the insurance they offer workers. In 2007, about forty-seven million Americans had no health insurance, even as the cost of medicine and medical care was rising.

Protecting the environment is another issue tied to the economy. Some industries say it costs too much for them to use methods that don't create pollution. U.S. leaders try to balance concern for the environment with other consider-ations. The country buys more than thirteen million barrels of oil every day from foreign countries. Most of this is used to power cars, heat homes, and fuel power plants. Some Americans have called for replacing oil with coal, which the United States can supply for itself. But mining operations can destroy the soil, and burning some kinds of coal cre-ates air pollution. The country continues to debate how to create enough power while doing the least damage to the environment.

Automobiles are a major cause of air pollution in the United States. In New York City, a toll has been sug-gested to try to limit the number of cars in the city.

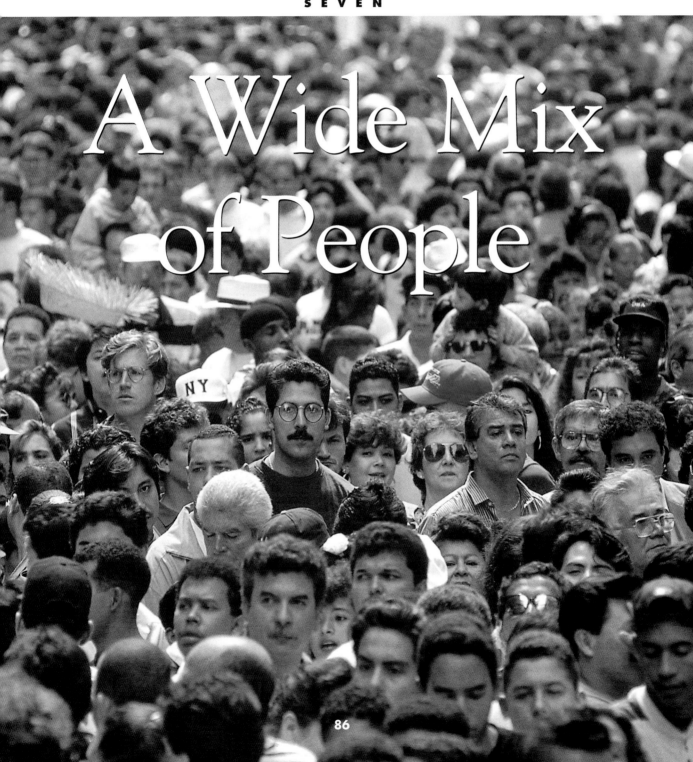

A Wide Mix of People

IN 1908, AN IMMIGRANT TO THE UNITED STATES NAMED Israel Zangwill wrote a play called *The Melting-Pot*. Zangwill described how people from many different nations and religious backgrounds "melted" together to form a new people—Americans. In the melting pot, immigrants learn to speak English and use American customs and, eventually, become citizens.

Years later, some scholars challenged the idea of the melting pot. They said that some newcomers remained distinct, keeping their native language and old customs. The United States was more like a salad bowl, with many different ingredients tossed together, than a melting pot.

Melting pot or salad bowl, no one argues that the United States is a land of great diversity. In its

Opposite: **A diverse crowd attends a street festival in New York City.**

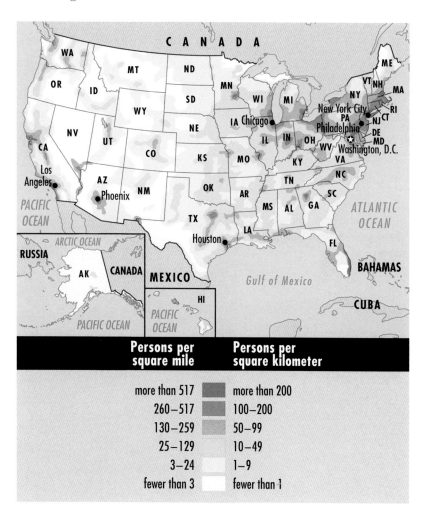

Persons per square mile	Persons per square kilometer
more than 517	more than 200
260–517	100–200
130–259	50–99
25–129	10–49
3–24	1–9
fewer than 3	fewer than 1

Population of the Largest U.S. Cities (2006 est.)

New York	8,214,426
Los Angeles	3,849,378
Chicago	2,833,321
Houston	2,144,491
Philadelphia	1,463,281
Phoenix	1,448,394

earliest days, many different groups of Native Americans developed. The first settlers included Europeans from different countries, as well as enslaved Africans. Today, U.S. citizens can trace their roots to almost every country in the world.

A Growing Nation

In June 2007, the estimated U.S. population was 302,205,826—and the number is growing all the time! Roughly 80 percent of all Americans live in urban areas, in or near cities.

In 2005, California had the highest population of any state, with 31.6 million people. The least-populated state was Wyoming, with 515,004 people. In general, states in the West and South are growing the fastest, while states in the Midwest and Northeast are growing more slowly. North Dakota saw its population decline between 2000 and 2005.

In California, huge housing developments have become more common as the population has grown.

A voting station in Santa Fe, New Mexico, directs voters with signs in both English and Spanish.

Who Speaks What?

Since the United States arose from thirteen British colonies, English has been the most common language in the nation. As of 2004, more than 216 million Americans spoke only English. Today, most immigrants learn some English, and their children study English in school. These youngsters may remain bilingual, able to speak two languages. Later generations are more likely to speak only English. In 2004, Spanish was the second most common language after English. About 30.5 million people spoke Spanish. Chinese was the next-most-common language, with 2.3 million speakers.

The Fastest-Growing States

In 2006, Arizona's population grew 3.6 percent—more than any other state's. It barely edged out neighboring Nevada as the fastest-growing state. Why do so many people head to these two states? Climate is part of the answer. Many people move to Arizona and Nevada to escape the cold, snowy winters found in much of the United States. These two states also have more affordable housing than California and other West Coast states.

A Wide Mix of People **89**

Gifts from Abroad

Here's a list of some English words with their roots in other languages:

English word	Foreign word	Language
cookie	*koekje*	Dutch
banjo	*mbanza*	Minbundu (an African language)
barbecue	*barbacoa*	Spanish/Taino Indian
squash (vegetable)	*askutasquash*	Narragansett Indian
pretzel	*brezel*	German
boondocks	*bundok*	Tagalog (a Philippine language)
galore	*go leor*	Irish (Gaelic)

On Native American reservations, children are again learning the languages of their ancestors. For many years, U.S. officials tried to make Native Americans speak only English, but now the tribes are trying to save languages that almost became extinct.

The Changing Face of America

At the time the United States was founded, most immigrants came from the British Isles and northern Europe. From the 1830s to the 1880s, Irish and Germans arrived in the greatest numbers. At the end of that century and until the 1920s, Italians and a variety of eastern Europeans became the most common newcomers. By 1910, almost 15 percent of all Americans had been born overseas.

In the last fifty years, the nature of immigration to the United States has changed. More of the new arrivals have come from Asia and Central and South America. Today, Hispanics are the largest minority group in the United States.

Ethnic Breakdown of the United States (2005 est.)

White	74.7%
Hispanic (can be any race)	14.5%
African American	12.1%
Asian American	4.3%
American Indian, Alaskan Native	0.8%
Native Hawaiian, Pacific Islander	0.1%
Two or more races	1.9%
Other	6.0%

Total is more than 100% because of rounding and because Hispanics can be any race.

More than forty-three million Americans trace their roots to Spanish-speaking countries such as Mexico, Cuba, and the Dominican Republic. Some have ties to Puerto Rico, which has been part of the United States since 1917. Asian Americans also have roots in many countries, including China, the Philippines, Vietnam, and India.

More than three hundred thousand Chinese Americans live in New York City.

Throughout history, many people in the United States have had mixed feelings about immigrants. Business owners often welcomed them because they filled jobs native-born Americans couldn't or wouldn't take. After wars, the United States opened its doors to refugees who lost their homes because of the fighting. But at times, immigrants who seemed too "foreign" have faced prejudice.

The first law restricting immigration was passed in 1882 and targeted the Chinese. Later laws limited Japanese immigrants and the number of people who came from southern and eastern Europe. An immigration law passed in 1965 made it easier for Asians and people from South and Central America to enter the United States. Since then, the number of legal immigrants to the country has never fallen below 300,000 a year.

In 1933, during the Great Depression, a group of unemployed Chinese American men protested to gain unemployment benefits for Asian Americans.

Not all immigrants come to the country legally. Each year, an estimated 850,000 people enter the United States illegally. Most are from Mexico and Central America and are seeking jobs so they can send money back to their families.

The presence of as many as 12 million illegal immigrants has sparked a huge debate across the country. Some people do not think the United States should provide education or health care to illegal immigrants. They also say that because the immigrants will work cheaply, they lower the wages paid to all workers. The immigrants and their defenders say that, as in the past, the newcomers are doing the hard, low-paying work that most Americans don't want to do.

Immigrants from all over world helped make the United States what it is today. The United States still has a strong pull on people around the world. Some people are willing to risk arrest or worse to try to come to the United States to build a better life.

In 2006, an estimated one hundred thousand people marched in Chicago, Illinois, to protest proposed immigration reforms.

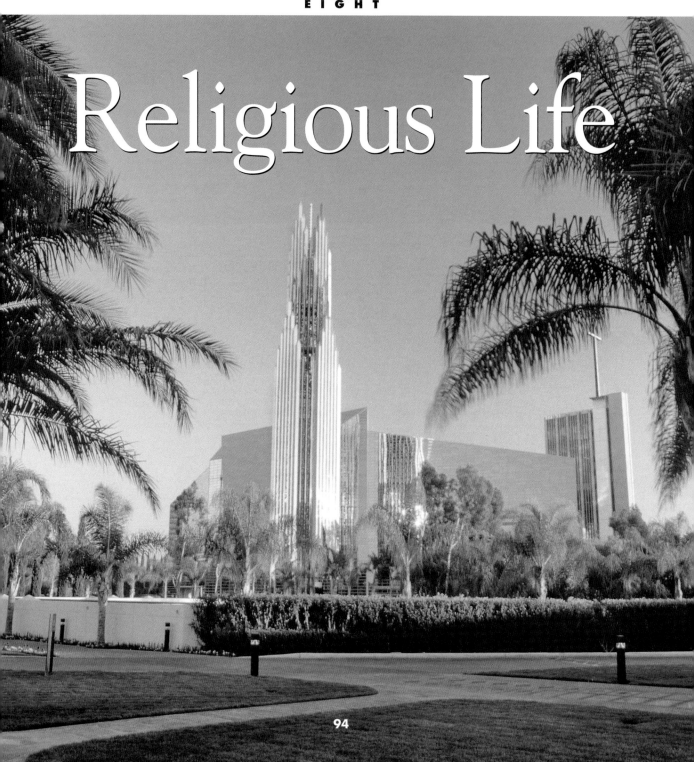

Religious Life

In 1630, John Winthrop led about a thousand Puritans from England to Massachusetts. He told the settlers they would build a "city on a hill" that would reflect the true teachings of the Christian faith. Winthrop and the other Puritans hoped their efforts would lead others to follow these teachings.

Religion was an important part of daily life for most colonists. By the time of the American Revolution, however, most American leaders did not want church rules to dominate the government, as they had with the Puritans. Instead, they wanted Americans to be free to worship as they chose, or to not worship at all. And they thought that the government should avoid seeming to favor any one religion. These ideas were later made part of the U.S. Constitution.

For millions of Americans, attending religious services remains important. Surveys show that between 20 and 40 percent of all Americans attend some kind of religious service every week. But millions more don't take part in religious services or follow the teachings of any one faith. American law and a general belief in letting others live as they choose has created a wide range of religious expression in the United States. For many, that means no religion at all.

Opposite: **The Crystal Cathedral in Garden Grove, California, is the headquarters of a televised evangelical ministry.**

Puritan leader John Winthrop stands aboard the *Arabella* before landing in Massachusetts in 1630.

Religions in the United States (2004)

Protestantism	53.0%
Roman Catholicism	23.4%
Judaism	2.0%
Other	7.3%
None	14.4%

Migrating Religions

Protestants dominated the British colonies and the early United States. Major groups include Baptists, Methodists, Lutherans, Presbyterians, and Episcopalians. At the time of the American Revolution, a small number of Jews and Roman Catholics lived in the British colonies. Spanish colonies such as Florida, California, and New Mexico were strongly Roman Catholic, because Catholicism was the national religion of Spain.

As immigrants poured into the United States, they brought their faiths with them. Orthodox Christians arrived from Greece, Russia, and parts of the Middle East. Millions of Jewish immigrants came from Russia, Poland, and other parts of Europe. The number of Roman Catholics rose through-

Early Religions

Every Native American group had strong religious beliefs. Although details varied, most tribes believed that a single powerful being or force created the universe. They also thought that all living things had spirits that lived after their physical form died. Even rocks and natural events such as weather could have spirits. Religious figures called shamans communicated between the spirit world and the world on Earth. Dances were an important part of religious rites. Some offered thanks to the spirits, while others sought their help.

After Europeans arrived in North America, they tried to force the Indians to give up their beliefs. Today, some Indians blend Christianity with traditional religious practices.

A Hindu temple in Calabasas, California

out the nineteenth and twentieth centuries, fueled first by the arrival of Irish and Germans, and then by Italians and Hispanics. Currently, Roman Catholics make up the largest single religious group in the United States, though all the different Protestant groups combined outnumber them.

Starting in the mid-nineteenth century, immigrants from Asia brought other faiths to the country, such as Buddhism and Hinduism. In recent years, Buddhists and Hindus have built huge temples for religious services, and Buddhism has won many converts in the United States. Islam is another fast-growing religion in the United States. Most American followers of Islam, called Muslims, are of African or Middle Eastern ancestry.

Muslim men attend a prayer service at the Islamic Center of South Jersey in Palmyra, New Jersey.

Islam has ties to both Christianity and Judaism. These three religions trace their roots back to the ancient Jewish leader Abraham, though they differ in their main beliefs. Muslims believe God sent Muhammad as his prophet to spread new, sacred teachings. Christians believe Jesus was the son of God. Jews believe that God is still waiting to send a messiah, or chosen person, to lead them in their faith.

Smaller Religious Groups

From its earliest days, America has seen smaller religious groups both arrive from overseas and develop here. The Society of Friends, or Quakers, is a small Protestant group that came from England in the 1650s. During the nineteenth century, Unitarianism developed in New England. Another home-grown faith is the Church of Christ, Scientist. Christian Scientists believe that God is divine love and that faith in God can cure the sick.

One of the world's fastest-growing religions is the Church of Jesus Christ of Latter-day Saints. Its believers are commonly called Mormons. New Yorker Joseph Smith founded the religion in 1840, but it truly blossomed in the desert of Utah, under the leadership of Brigham Young.

Some of the less common faiths brought to the United States include Baha'i, which arose in Persia (now Iran) in the nineteenth century. Its followers believe that all human religions are the expression of one universal faith. Wicca has roots among the Celts, who once lived in the British Isles and western Europe. Wiccans worship a God and a Goddess and feel close to nature.

The Mormon Salt Lake Temple is located in the center of Salt Lake City, Utah, on a block known as Temple Square.

Filled with the Holy Spirit

The Assemblies of God is one of the fastest-growing evangelical faiths. In 2005, it had almost 2.8 million members in the United States. The Assemblies of God is part of the evangelical movement called Pentecostalism. Pentecostal churches fill their services with emotion and music. Some followers believe that their faith can cure the sick or give people the power to speak languages they don't know. This is called "speaking in tongues." Many other born-again Christians reject the beliefs of the Pentecostals.

"Born Again"

In recent decades, some Protestant ministers have encouraged worshippers to return to what they consider the true faith. This means declaring a renewed personal belief that Jesus Christ is the son of God, sent to save the souls of humans. People who do this are sometimes called born-again Christians. They are also sometimes called evangelical or fundamentalist Christians. In recent decades, they have played a major role in U.S. politics. They typically support prayer in public schools and want to outlaw abortion. In general, evangelical or fundamentalist groups are growing faster than other churches in America today.

Religion in Daily Life

Religious services often help people feel like they are part of a community. They know they share ideas with others and can count on these people in times of need. Religion has sometimes also taken on a larger social and political role in the United States. Immigrants rely on services to give them a tie to their homeland. Religious leaders have helped newcomers find jobs and places to live. Religious organizations have also set up schools to educate children.

An Arena of Worship

Houston's Compaq Center once hosted professional basketball games. Since 2005, it's been known as the Lakewood Church. With room for sixteen thousand worshippers, it's the largest church in the United States.

Lakewood is a nondenominational Christian church, meaning it is not tied to any one set of Protestant beliefs. Joel Osteen, a popular speaker and writer on religious issues, runs the church.

Religion and the community of churches have helped many African Americans withstand prejudice. African American religious leaders such as Martin Luther King Jr. led the fight for equal rights and better living conditions.

Fighting for Change, Peacefully

Martin Luther King Jr. took his message of brotherly love and equality from the church to the streets. Like his father, he trained to be a Baptist minister. But starting in 1955, King also became a leader of the civil rights movement—the effort to give African Americans full legal rights. He led marches and protests in several southern cities, including Birmingham and Selma, Alabama. In 1963, he gave his famous "I Have a Dream" speech, calling for racial equality. King believed in using peaceful methods to effect change. King was still fighting for civil rights when he was shot and killed in Memphis, Tennessee, in 1968.

In 1838, the governor of Missouri signed an order expelling Mormons from the state.

The major religions of the world often preach the "golden rule"—treat people the way you would like them to treat you. At different times in U.S. history, however, followers of one faith have struck out against believers of another. During the nineteenth century, many Protestants thought that Roman Catholics could not be good citizens. The Protestants feared that Catholics would be more loyal to their religious leader,

A Declining Role for Religion?

The United States has seen a lot of changes in religion over the past few decades. The traditional Protestant churches, such as Episcopalian, Lutheran, Methodist, and Presbyterian, have seen their membership fall. Some people leave to join fundamentalist churches. Others join completely different religions. Some stop attending church altogether. A 2001 survey showed this decline. A little more than 76 percent of Americans called themselves Christians. A decade earlier, the number was 86 percent. In 2001, the number of people who said that they do not belong to any religion was 14 percent, almost double what it was in 1990.

the pope, than to elected political leaders. Jews, both in the United States and around the world, have faced intolerance. Among Protestants, groups have disagreed on whether or not members must be "born again" to go to heaven.

Since the September 11, 2001, terrorist attacks, Muslims have been targeted for their beliefs. The terrorists followed a fundamentalist branch of Islam that does not tolerate other faiths. Some Americans have associated all Muslims with these narrow beliefs. According to a 2006 poll, about 40 percent of Americans say they have some prejudice against Muslims. Muslim leaders have tried to show that most American Muslims are patriotic citizens. The Islamic Networks Group, for example, sends speakers around the country to schools, businesses, and other organizations to promote understanding between Muslims and followers of other faiths.

Some American Muslims have gone to great lengths to counteract the discrimination against Muslims that has grown since the attacks of September 11, 2001.

Talent of All Kinds

HOLLYWOOD

THE FIRST EUROPEAN SETTLERS IN NORTH AMERICA DID not have much time for arts and recreation. Their lives were spent planting fields and making the goods they needed to survive. But over time, Americans showed skill as artists, writers, actors, and musicians. They also developed or adapted sports that have become huge industries.

Opposite: **Hollywood, California, is the center of the American film industry.**

The first Bible printed in North America was made in Cambridge, Massachusetts, in 1663.

A Flair for Writing

For the Puritans and other early European settlers, the Bible was the most important book they possessed. The first writings published in America were religious.

The nineteenth century saw an explosion of literary talent in the United States. Famous American poets of the time include Emily Dickinson, who rarely left her Massachusetts home, and Walt Whitman, who wrote about common people and daily life. His collection of poems called *Leaves of Grass* influenced many later writers. Novelists also made their mark. Herman Melville is most famous for *Moby-Dick*, the story of the hunt

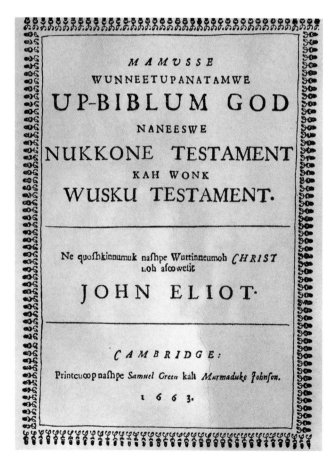

Novelist Herman Melville was born on August 1, 1819, in New York City.

for a great white whale. Harriet Beecher Stowe used real life as a model for *Uncle Tom's Cabin*, a novel about slavery. Henry James spent much of his life in Europe, but he wrote about his fellow Americans in his novels.

Modern Writers

In the twentieth century, great U.S. novelists wrote in many different styles. Ernest Hemingway favored short sentences describing the lives of men of action. His most famous book is *The Sun Also Rises*. William Faulkner used a style called stream of consciousness, which reflects a character's inner

An American Master

Two of the best-loved characters in U.S. fiction are Tom Sawyer and Huck Finn. These two fun-loving boys were the creation of Missouri native Samuel Clemens (1835–1910), who wrote under the name Mark Twain. Twain's books are filled with humor, but he also makes serious comments about human faults and life in the United States. *The Adventures of Huckleberry Finn* is considered one of the greatest American novels.

thoughts. Faulkner detailed life in his native South, and his works include *As I Lay Dying* and *The Sound and the Fury*. Both men won the Nobel Prize for Literature, the world's highest honor for writers.

Other American Nobel Prize winners include the poet T. S. Eliot and the playwright Eugene O'Neill. Eliot was known for his complex poems. O'Neill wrote about his own family life in *Long Day's Journey into Night*. A more recent Nobel Prize winner is Toni Morrison. Her work explores the experiences of African Americans. Her best-known work is the 1987 novel *Beloved*.

American writers have also produced many great stories for children. Theodore Geisel, better known as Doctor Seuss, wrote and drew funny rhyming books such as *The Cat in the Hat* and *How the Grinch Stole Christmas*. One of the most popular children's books ever is *Charlotte's Web*, by E. B. White.

Above left: **The works of William Faulkner reflected the culture of his home state of Mississippi.**

Above right: **Poet, critic, and playwright T. S. Eliot won the Nobel Prize for Literature in 1948.**

Meet at the Met

Each year, more than five million people pass through the doors of New York's Metropolitan Museum of Art, one of the largest art museums in the world. When the museum was founded in 1870, it had just 174 paintings. Today, the Met owns more than 2 million pieces of art, some of them three hundred thousand years old! The collection comes from around the world, but the Met also has a wide range of American art, including many examples of the Hudson River School of painting.

Monte Video, by Thomas Cole. Cole was a leading member of the Hudson River School.

Art for the Eye

Many of the early famous painters in the United States produced portraits of other Americans. Others depicted scenes in the country's history. John Singleton Copley, Gilbert Stuart, and John Trumbull are some of these painters. The Hudson River School movement arose in the early nineteenth century. Its members, such as Thomas Cole and Frederic Edwin Church, painted large, colorful scenes of the Hudson River valley and other beautiful spots in the Northeast.

Through the nineteenth century, American painters blended skills learned in Europe with U.S. scenes. Winslow Homer spent time overseas before coming back to the United States. He is famous for water scenes set along the Atlantic Coast. Mary Cassatt went to Paris and learned the style of painting called impressionism. It is called that because the artist paints his or her impressions of or feelings about a subject rather than showing exactly how it looks.

Creating Modern Art

The twentieth century saw artists looking for new ways to express themselves. They wanted to reflect the energy—and sometimes chaos—of a fast-changing, industrialized world. U.S. painters in particular shaped art after World War II. Jackson Pollock became famous for dripping different colors of paint in wild patterns or throwing the paint onto the canvas. Willem de Kooning, a Dutch immigrant, painted people and objects, but they could barely be seen as such. Other artists continued to paint recognizable subjects. Georgia O'Keeffe became famous for her huge paintings of flowers and scenes of desert life.

In the 1960s, a group of U.S. artists burst forth with "pop art." They took subjects from everyday life—comic books, soup cans, newspaper photos—and treated them as art. Andy Warhol, Robert Rauschenberg, and Roy Lichtenstein were among the leaders of the pop art movement.

Andy Warhol was known for incorporating images of everyday items in his art. *Black Bean* was part of his Soup Can Series I.

Photography, invented during the nineteenth century, became a true art form during the 1900s. Some of the great American photographers were Ansel Adams, Dorothea Lange, and Edward Steichen.

Architecture and Sculpture

Among the great early architects in the United States was President Thomas Jefferson, who is famous for designing his Virginia home, Monticello. Toward the end of the nineteenth century, Louis Sullivan and Daniel Burnham of Chicago helped create some of the world's first skyscrapers. Frank Lloyd Wright was perhaps the greatest U.S. architect. He favored simple, geometric shapes and low, flat homes. His Fallingwater, in Pennsylvania, is a house built over a brook so that the water flows through it.

Many people consider Fallingwater in Mill Run, Pennsylvania, to be architect Frank Lloyd Wright's masterpiece.

The most famous American sculptor of the nineteenth century was Augustus Saint-Gaudens. Some of his designs were used on U.S. coins. After World War II, U.S. sculptors moved away from showing people or identifiable objects. Instead, Alexander Calder made colorful mobiles, and Isamu Noguchi designed lamps and abstract statues.

Augustus Saint-Gaudens made this golden sculpture of General William Tecumseh Sherman, which stands in Central Park in New York City.

Making Music

The United States has produced several renowned composers. Aaron Copland combined distinctly American themes and musical styles with classical music. In one of his works, he wrote the music for a ballet about the Old West outlaw Billy the Kid. Leonard Bernstein also combined classical training with more popular styles. Most Americans know him as the composer of the music for such beloved musicals as *West Side Story*.

Elvis Presley had eighteen number-one hits during his career. He also starred in thirty-one films.

American musicians have made their greatest impact in popular music. Jazz, blues, rock and roll, country, hip-hop—all were created in the United States. Most of these styles drew on the experiences of African Americans who blended European styles of music with African musical traditions to create the blues and jazz. In churches, African Americans used these musical styles to sing about God, leading to gospel music. During the 1950s, young white musicians learned the blues and rhythm and blues, which usually featured horns and danceable beats. Some, such as Elvis Presley, then blended those styles with country and bluegrass, which had their roots in the folk music that Scottish, Irish, and English immigrants brought with them to the South. In the 1960s, Bob Dylan combined intense, mysterious lyrics, a biting attitude, and folk tunes to become the voice of his generation. Hip-hop was created in the streets of New York in the late 1970s as young blacks looked for a new way to describe their lives.

In jazz, the greatest names include trumpeters Louis Armstrong and Miles Davis, composers Duke Ellington and Charles Mingus, and saxophonists Charlie Parker and John Coltrane. Some of the great American singers also worked in jazz, including Ella Fitzgerald and Frank Sinatra. Many jazz artists perform their own version of popular songs by the composers George and Ira Gershwin and Cole Porter. Today, popular musicians of all fields borrow from one another, keeping the American music scene vibrant and ever-changing.

On the Screen

Motion pictures are made around the world, but when it comes to big, splashy films, most people think of Hollywood. Since the 1920s, that section of Los Angeles has been the capital of the movie industry. Films made there have helped spread American culture, values, and language to every part

Lucille Ball is best known for her television show, *I Love Lucy*, which aired from 1951 to 1957.

of the globe. Making movies is big business. In 2006, Americans spent almost US$10 billion to see movies at their local theaters, and more than double that to watch videos at home.

Starting in the 1950s, television became a popular form of entertainment. Reruns shown on cable TV have kept alive many of the classic shows, such as *I Love Lucy*. As with films, American TV shows run around the world. They are usually dubbed, with actors saying the lines in the local languages.

Action-Packed Entertainment

Americans love sports of all kinds, and they take professional and college athletics very seriously. Baseball, or games like it, have been played in the United States since the days of the American Revolution. Today, baseball is called the "national pastime" of the United States. In 2006, almost seventy-six million fans came out to root for their favorite Major League team. Many terms have made their way from baseball into everyday conversation. "Pinch-hitting" means filling in for someone else, and "playing hardball"—hardball is a nickname for baseball—means getting tough or serious.

Johnny Damon of the New York Yankees smacks the ball in a game against the Boston Red Sox.

Football is a popular sport at both college and pro levels. Each year, the champion of the National Football League is crowned in the Super Bowl. Basketball was invented in Springfield, Massachusetts, in 1891, and it's now hugely popular around the world. Soccer is not a popular spectator sport in the United States, but more than three million boys and girls play in organized soccer leagues each year.

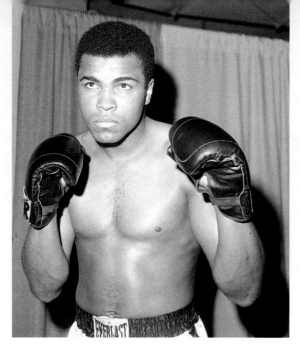

The Greatest

Perhaps the best-known U.S. sports figure ever is former heavyweight boxing champion Muhammad Ali. Born Cassius Clay, Ali had fast hands in the ring and a way with words out of it. He often told fans, "I am the greatest!" Ali faced problems during the 1960s when he joined a religious group called the Nation of Islam and refused to serve in the Vietnam War. The Nation of Islam held some traditional Muslim beliefs but also condemned "devilish" whites for their actions toward blacks. By the 1970s, however, Ali was once again a popular figure. Ali now follows the traditional teachings of Islam and works for peace and understanding among people of all backgrounds. A center devoted to those efforts and his boxing career opened in his hometown of Louisville, Kentucky, in 2005.

Popular individual sports are golf and tennis. Many people consider Tiger Woods the greatest golfer ever. Woods hit his first hole-in-one when he was six years old, and his talent has just kept improving. Through 2007, he had won thirteen "Grand Slam" events, the top tournaments in professional golf.

Tiger Woods is one of the most successful professional golfers of all time.

Daily Life

THE UNITED STATES HAS MORE THAN THREE HUNDRED million people from many different backgrounds and with many different interests. It's impossible to define the "typical" American. Yet, like other people around the world, Americans have certain needs and desires: food and shelter; time for friends, family, and fun. And despite their differences, Americans share a way of life admired by many around the world.

Opposite: **Single-family homes, such as these in Moorestown, New Jersey, are common in the United States.**

At Home and on the Road

For many Americans, owning a home is an important part of the American Dream. A little less than 70 percent of American house-holds live in a house or apartment that they own. Most of the others rent or share housing with relatives. About 2 to 3 percent of Americans are homeless for at least one night in any given five-year period. Some don't have jobs; while others work but can't afford housing near their jobs. Many cities and towns provide shelters to help the homeless.

Homeless men and women eat at a soup kitchen in New York City.

Americans prefer detached, single-family homes with yards. American homes have been getting larger since the 1980s, even as the size of the average family has fallen. Most large houses are located in suburbs outside cities. As suburbs grow, land becomes more expensive and people build even farther out, in areas called exurbs.

The growth of suburbs has made the United States a car-oriented society. So has a love of the freedom cars provide. About nine out of ten adult Americans own a car. No other country in the world has as high a percentage of car owners. In some suburbs, garages that hold three or four cars have become common. Workers who drive to their jobs spend an average of fifty minutes each day on the road.

An extensive highway system crisscrosses the United States.

Rules of the Road

Cars are part of life in the United States, but they can be dangerous. More than forty-two thousand people died in car crashes in 2005. All states have passed laws to try to make the roads safer. Most states require that drivers be at least age sixteen before they get a license, and more states are placing restrictions on when teens can drive. North Carolina, for example, does not let teens drive after 9:00 p.m. As of 2007, twenty-four states had laws that let police officers pull over people not wearing seat belts. And states are increasing penalties for people who drink alcohol and then drive.

From Kindergarten to College

To get their jobs, U.S. workers need training. Students go to either public school, which is free, or private school. Students usually begin elementary school at age five or six and complete high school at about age eighteen. After graduating from high school, some students go to technical schools that focus on specific skills, such as fixing computers or cars.

Fifth graders attend a math class in Woodbridge, New Jersey.

The United States also has many colleges and universities. In 2005, almost eighteen million students were enrolled at colleges. Leading private universities in the country include Yale, in New Haven, Connecticut; Harvard, in Cambridge, Massachusetts; and Stanford, in Palo Alto, California. Top public universities are found in Michigan, California, and Texas, among other states.

New York City is famous for its pizza.

Fantastic Foods

In their homes and on the road, Americans enjoy eating a variety of foods. The many different ethnic groups that have come to America have contributed to the nation's cuisine. Hamburgers and hot dogs trace their roots to Germany, pizza comes from Italy, salsa is from Mexico, peanuts were first grown in Africa. One truly native dish is popcorn, which the Indians introduced to European settlers centuries ago.

Americans invented the notion of fast food. McDonald's, a U.S. corporation, is the world's largest fast-food company. The fast-food giant and its competitors are sometimes criticized for selling unhealthy food. Some diseases that are on the rise, such as diabetes and heart disease, can be traced to diet. As some Americans try to eat foods with less fat and sugar, the menus at some fast-food restaurants are changing to reflect this demand.

Crazy About Coffee

Americans once threw tea into Boston Harbor to protest British taxes. Today, coffee has replaced tea as the most popular hot beverage, and Howard Schultz played a large role in that. In 1987, Schultz bought a Seattle coffee company called Starbucks. By the mid-1990s, he had turned Starbucks into an international chain of stores selling high-priced coffee drinks. In 2006, Starbucks opened more than seven hundred new shops in the United States alone, and the company brewed 277 million gallons of coffee each day around the world. Thanks to the success of Starbucks, Schultz is now a billionaire.

Giving Thanks

One menu that's particularly American is the typical Thanksgiving Day meal. Thanksgiving traces its roots to the 1621 celebration the Pilgrims of Plymouth shared with the Wampanoag Indians. Today's Thanksgiving table typically features turkey, stuffing, gravy, mashed potatoes, and cranberry sauce. Members of different ethnic groups may add some of their native dishes, too, but the bird is the star of the meal. Apple and pumpkin pies are usually served for dessert.

The United States was also the birthplace of the first TV dinner, a ready-made frozen meal that was heated up in the oven. Today, microwaves and frozen foods help keep active people fed, while others munch snacks such as potato chips and energy bars while they're on the go. A more relaxed way to dine is cooking outside on the grill. In 2005, almost twelve million adults said they cooked outside at least twice a week.

Many Americans love to grill. Popular grilled foods include hamburgers, hot dogs, and kebabs.

Time to Relax

When it's time to take a break from working, Americans pursue a wide range of pastimes. In 2002, top activities included attending sporting events, playing sports or exercising, going to the movies, gardening, hanging out with friends and family, and working with charities. Watching TV, however, is the top form of recreation. In 2005, adult Americans reported watching an average of 2.6 hours every day.

Computers have changed how people around the world live, and Americans are ranked among the top computer users. In 2007, an estimated 211 million Americans used the Internet at home, school, or work. With the Internet, they can stay in touch with friends, post their own writings and art in blogs, download music, and do research. Many younger Americans also use computers to play video games.

Young baseball fans reach for a ball during a game in Oakland, California.

Seeing Double

When the English came to New Amsterdam (New York City), they saw the Dutch playing a game with two ropes. The English called the game double Dutch. Today, this jump-rope game is still popular. To play, the turners rotate one rope clockwise and the other counter-clockwise at the same time. One rope is going up while the other is going down. The turners recite rhymes or songs while the jumper tries to skip over the ropes without stumbling. At times, two jumpers may go at once. The best jumpers can do cartwheels and other stunts in between the ropes.

Let's Go!

The United States is blessed with natural beauty and offers people many choices for enjoying the great outdoors. The country has fifty-five national parks, where mining, hunting, and other activities are prohibited. Yellowstone, which lies mostly in Wyoming, became the nation's first national park in 1872. The U.S. National Park Service runs national parks, national monuments, and other sites noted for their historical importance or unique physical beauty. These spots are popular tourist attractions, drawing more than 272 million visitors in 2006.

Tourists get a guided tour of coral reefs in a glass-bottomed boat.

Each state also has its own parks set aside to preserve nature, honor the past, and provide outdoor recreation, such as camping, fishing, and boating. Florida has the country's first underwater park, John Pennekamp Coral Reef State Park. Visitors can float in its warm waters to see the reefs up close, or look at them through a glass-bottom boat.

Millions of Americans seek out another kind of park—amusement parks. Rides, games, and food provide fun-filled days at amusement parks across the country. Coney Island, one of the most famous parks, opened in Brooklyn, New York, in 1895. Related to amusement parks are theme parks, which often include water slides or movies. Walt Disney World in Florida and the nearby Epcot Center are among the most popular theme parks in the world.

Celebrations of All Kinds

For most Americans, holidays and festivals provide a welcome break from the routines of work and school. Some holidays are tied to specific religions. Christmas and Easter are important Christian holidays. The German practice of decorating a tree inside the home became popular in the United States during the mid-nineteenth century. After church services on Christmas and Easter, families usually celebrate with large meals. Food also

The Christmas tree is a celebrated tradition in the United States. Many families who are not religious still decorate their houses with one.

National Holidays

New Year's Day	January 1
Martin Luther King Day	Third Monday in January
Presidents' Day	Third Monday in February
Memorial Day	Last Monday in May
Independence Day	July 4
Labor Day	First Monday in September
Columbus Day	Second Monday in October
Veterans Day	November 11
Thanksgiving Day	Fourth Thursday in November
Christmas	December 25

plays a role in a major Jewish holiday, Passover. During Passover, families gather and eat foods associated with the Jews' escape from slavery in Egypt more than three thousand years ago. Muslims are required to refrain from eating during daylight hours in the Muslim month of Ramadan. At the end of Ramadan, they enjoy a three-day celebration called 'Id al-Fitr. A major Hindu celebration is Diwali. For five days, people honor different Hindu gods and light lamps to show the triumph of good over evil.

Not all holidays in the United States are tied to religion. January 1, New Year's Day, welcomes the arrival of a new year. The night before is a time of huge parties, as people wait for the clock to strike midnight. Some ethnic and religious groups follow different calendars, so their new year comes on different days. Vietnamese and Chinese Americans celebrate their new year in January or February. In some Asian American neighborhoods, the new year is celebrated with fireworks and parades.

Dragons are traditional at parades celebrating Chinese New Year.

Some of the most important U.S. holidays honor historical figures and events. Memorial Day honors Americans killed in wars, and Veterans Day recognizes the bravery of all the men and women who have served in the military. Christopher Columbus has his own day in honor of his historic voyages to the Americas. And Martin Luther King Day celebrates King's efforts to win equality for African Americans and others.

Of all the historical holidays, the most widely celebrated is probably Independence Day—the Fourth of July. The day marks the signing of the Declaration of Independence in 1776. The festivities often start with parades. Then, friends and families gather for picnics. At night, fireworks fill the sky. The day reminds Americans of the freedom they have, and of the amazing country they and their ancestors have built.

Fireworks explode over New York City in celebration of Independence Day.

Timeline

United States History

Native Americans leave behind tools later discovered in Virginia.	**ca. 16,000 years ago**
Native Americans of the Southwest begin farming.	**ca. 1500** B.C.
The Mississippian city of Cahokia reaches a population of perhaps 20,000.	A.D. **1150**
Spanish explorer Juan Ponce de Léon reaches Florida.	1513
Spanish settlers bring African slaves to South Carolina.	1526
The Spanish found the first permanent settlement in what became the United States in St. Augustine, Florida.	1565
The first permanent English settlement is founded in Jamestown, Virginia.	1607
Plymouth, Massachusetts, is founded by English settlers later called Pilgrims.	1620
The French and Indian War ends.	1763
The American Revolution begins.	1775
The Declaration of Independence is adopted.	1776

World History

2500 B.C.	Egyptians build the pyramids and the Sphinx in Giza.
563 B.C.	The Buddha is born in India.
A.D. 313	The Roman emperor Constantine legalizes Christianity.
610	The Prophet Muhammad begins preaching a new religion called Islam.
1054	The Eastern (Orthodox) and Western (Roman Catholic) Churches break apart.
1095	The Crusades begin.
1215	King John seals the Magna Carta.
1300s	The Renaissance begins in Italy.
1347	The plague sweeps through Europe.
1453	Ottoman Turks capture Constantinople, conquering the Byzantine Empire.
1492	Columbus arrives in North America.
1500s	Reformers break away from the Catholic Church, and Protestantism is born.
1776	The U.S. Declaration of Independence is signed.

United States History

The U.S. Constitution is written.	1787
The Louisiana Purchase doubles the size of the United States.	1803
The United States wins control of California and other southwestern lands from Mexico.	1848
The Civil War begins.	1861
The Civil War ends and slavery is abolished.	1865
The United States enters World War I.	1917
The 19th Amendment gives women the right to vote.	1920
The Great Depression begins.	1929
After the Japanese attack Pearl Harbor, Hawai'i, the United States enters World War II.	1941
World War II ends.	1945
As part of the cold war, U.S. troops fight in Korea.	1950
Martin Luther King Jr. emerges as a leader of the civil rights movement.	1955
U.S. combat troops arrive in Vietnam.	1965
Terrorists attack New York and Washington, D.C.; the United States invades Afghanistan in retaliation.	2001
The United States goes to war with Iraq.	2003
Hurricane Katrina destroys large sections of New Orleans, Louisiana.	2005

World History

1789	The French Revolution begins.
1865	The American Civil War ends.
1879	The first practical light bulb is invented.
1914	World War I begins.
1917	The Bolshevik Revolution brings communism to Russia.
1929	A worldwide economic depression begins.
1939	World War II begins.
1945	World War II ends.
1957	The Vietnam War begins.
1969	Humans land on the Moon.
1975	The Vietnam War ends.
1989	The Berlin Wall is torn down as communism crumbles in Eastern Europe.
1991	The Soviet Union breaks into separate states.
2001	Terrorists attack the World Trade Center in New York City and the Pentagon in Washington, D.C.

Fast Facts

Official name: United States of America

Capital: Washington, D.C.

Official language: None, though English is dominant

U.S. Capitol

U.S. flag

Great Plains

Official religion:	None
Year of founding:	The Declaration of Independence was adopted on July 4, 1776
National anthem:	"The Star-Spangled Banner"
Type of government:	Federal republic
Chief of state:	President
Head of government:	President
Area:	3,619,969 square miles (9,375,677 sq km)
Bordering countries:	Mexico and Canada
Highest elevation:	Mount McKinley, Alaska, 20,320 feet (6,194 m) above sea level
Lowest elevation:	Death Valley, California, 282 feet (86 m) below sea level
Highest recorded temperature:	134°F (57°C), Death Valley, California, July 10, 1913
Lowest recorded temperature:	−80°F (−62°C),Prospect Creek Camp, Endicott Mountains, Alaska, January 23, 1971
Highest average annual precipitation:	460 inches (1,168 cm), Mount Waialeale, Hawai'i
Lowest average annual precipitation:	1.6 inches (4 cm), Cow Creek, California

Statue of Liberty

National population (2007 est.): 302,205,826

Population of largest cities (2006 est.):

New York City	8,214,426
Los Angeles	3,849,378
Chicago	2,833,321
Houston	2,144,491
Philadelphia	1,463,281
Phoenix	1,448,394

Famous landmarks:
- ▶ *White House*, Washington, D.C.
- ▶ *Lincoln Memorial*, Washington, D.C.
- ▶ *Vietnam Veterans Memorial*, Washington, D.C.
- ▶ *Statue of Liberty*, New York City
- ▶ *Grand Canyon*, Arizona
- ▶ *Great Lakes*, United States–Canada border

Industry: The United States manufactures such large items as automobiles, electronics, and industrial equipment, as well as chemicals and food products. It exports raw materials, food, and finished goods to markets around the world. The nation also has a large service industry in the health, financial, communications, tourism, and retail fields. Major agricultural products include corn, cattle, and milk.

Currency: The U.S. dollar, which is divided into 100 cents.

Weights and measures: The common system

Literacy rate (2003): 99%

Currency

Americans

Harriet Tubman

Famous Americans:

Muhammad Ali	(1942–)
Boxer	
Susan B. Anthony	(1820–1906)
Leader of the women's suffrage movement	
Louis Armstrong	(1901–1971)
Jazz musician	
Thomas Edison	(1847–1931)
Inventor	
Henry Ford	(1863–1947)
Automaker	
Thomas Jefferson	(1743–1826)
President and author of the Declaration of Independence	
Martin Luther King Jr.	(1929–1968)
Civil rights leader	
Abraham Lincoln	(1809–1865)
President during the Civil War	
Tisquantum (Squanto)	(ca. 1590–1622)
Indian who helped the Pilgrims	
Harriet Tubman	(ca. 1820–1913)
Former slave who led other slaves to freedom	
Mark Twain (Samuel Clemens)	(1835–1910)
Author and humorist	
George Washington	(1732–1799)
Revolutionary War hero and the first president	

To Find Out More

Books

▷ Burgan, Michael. *Cold War.* 4 vols. Austin, TX: Raintree Steck-Vaughn Publishers, 2001.

▷ Dolan, Edward F. *The American Indian Wars.* Brookfield, CT: Millbrook Press, 2003.

▷ Finkelman, Paul. *The Constitution.* Washington, DC: National Geographic Society, 2006.

▷ Hakim, Joy. *A History of US.* New York: Oxford University Press, 2005.

▷ Laezman, Rick. *100 Hispanic Americans Who Changed History.* Milwaukee: World Almanac Library, 2005.

▷ Masoff, Joy. *We Are All Americans: Understanding Diversity.* Waccabuc, NY: Five Ponds Press, 2006.

▷ McPherson, James. *Fields of Fury: The American Civil War.* New York: Atheneum Books for Young Readers, 2002.

▷ McWhorter, Diane. *A Dream of Freedom: The Civil Rights Movement from 1954 to 1968.* New York: Scholastic, 2004.

▷ Miller, Brandon Marie. *Declaring Independence: Life During the American Revolution.* Minneapolis: Lerner, 2005.

▷ Sirimarco, Elizabeth. *The Time of Slavery.* New York: Benchmark Books, 2007.

▷ Stefoff, Rebecca. *Growth in America, 1865–1914.* New York: Benchmark Books, 2003.

▷ Worth, Richard. *Colonial America: Building Toward Independence.* Berkeley Heights, NJ: Enslow, 2006.

Video

▷ *Americana: Beginnings.* TMW Media Group, 2004.

▷ *The Declaration of Independence.* Goldhill Video, 2004.

- *Our Federal Government.* 100% Educational Videos, 2004.

- *Sea to Shining Sea.* Educate Media Resources, 2006.

Web Sites

- Digital History—
  Primary Source Documents
  www.digitalhistory.uh.edu/documents/
  documents_p1.cfm
  For an amazing number of original documents from U.S. history.

- **Kids.gov—The Official Kids' Portal for the U.S. Government**
  www.kids.gov/
  To learn all about the U.S. government and U.S. history.

- **PBS—U.S. History**
  www.pbs.org/history/history_
  united.html
  For a variety of in-depth stories about important people and events in U.S. history.

- **The World Factbook—
  United States**
  https://www.cia.gov/library/
  publications/the-world-factbook/
  geos/us.html
  For a ton of quick facts about the United States.

Organizations and Embassies

- **The Embassy of the United States of America**
  490 Sussex Drive
  Ottawa, Ontario K1N 1G8
  613/238-5335
  ottawa.usembassy.gov

- **Smithsonian Institution**
  Washington, DC 20013
  www.si.edu

- **U.S. Census Bureau**
  United States Department of Commerce
  Washington, DC 20230
  www.census.gov

Index

Meet the Author

FOR ALMOST TWENTY YEARS, MICHAEL BURGAN HAS TRIED to help children understand the world around them, first as an editor at the Weekly Reader Corporation and then as a freelance author. He has written more than 150 books for kids, mostly about U.S. history and geography. His work on the America the Beautiful series for Scholastic provided him with background for writing this book about the United States. So did his travels around the country, from New England to California and many states in between. (New Mexico is his favorite, and he hopes to live there someday.) In writing this book, Burgan relied on the Internet for the most up-to-date statistics and for news that is not often reported in the major media. He also consulted books written by expert historians and scientists to round out his view of the United States.

A native of Glastonbury, Connecticut, Burgan has loved exploring the United States since his first travels to New York City and Boston as a child. He now lives in Chicago with his wife, Samantha, and the Windy City has been a perfect base for visiting sites and cities across the Midwest. When he's not writing for children, Burgan enjoys the theater. He has written several plays.

Photo Credits

Photographs © 2008:

age fotostock: 28 (Walter Bibikow/Jon Arnold Images), 25 top (Corbis), 108 top (Kord.com), 110 (José Fuste Raga), 24 (Lin Sutherland)

Alamy Images: 86, 133 top (Phil Degginger), 20 top (Erin Paul Donovan), 37 (Jon Gardey/Robert Harding Picture Library Ltd), 91 (Jeff Greenberg), 22 (Interfoto Pressebildagentur), 74, 130 (Jon Arnold Images), 16 (David Muenker), 79 (Chuck Pefley), 116 (Ted Pink), 84 (Fredrik Renander) Alaska Stock Images: 32 (Steven Kazlowski), 7 bottom, 36 bottom (Don Pitcher)

AP Images: 70 top (Charles Rex Arbogast), 98 (Mike Derer), 68 (Charles Dharapak), 81 (Ford Motor Co.), 96 (Bill Hefton), 34 top (Steve Helber), 103 (Beth A. Keiser), 124 (Mickey Krakowski), 82 (Paul Sakuma), 31 (Bill Wagner/The Daily News)

Art Resource, NY: 109 (Tate Gallery, London, Great Britian/© Copyright Warhol Foundation for the Visual Arts/ Artists Rights Scoiety (ARS), NY)

Corbis Images: 65 (Seab Adair/Reuters), 107 left (ANSA), 104 (Craig Aurness), 17 (Tom Bean), 12, 43, 55, 62, 92, 95, 107 right, 115 top (Bettmann), 80 (Jonathan Blair), 115 bottom (Matt Campbell/ epa), 118 (Ron Chapple), 89 (Steven Clevenger), 94 (Philip James Corwin), 119 bottom (Aristide Economopoulos/ Star Ledger), 13 (Owen Franken), 9 (Lewis Wickes Hine/Bettmann), 111 (Jack Hollingsworth), 120 (Thomas A. Kelly), 83 (Kim Kulish), 21, 131 (Larry Lee Photography), 26, 30 (Danny Lehman), 121 top (Becky Luigart-Stayner), 122 (John G. Mabanglo/epa), 108 bottom (Francis G. Mayer), 117 (Viviane Moos), 19, 42 (David Muench), 29 (Eric Nguyen), 126 (Douglas Peebles), 102 (H.R. Robinson), 88 (Bob Sacha), 63 (Steve Schapiro), 101 (Flip Schulke), 97 (Joseph Sohm/Visions of America), 66 (Junius Brutus Stearns/Bettmann), 112 (Sunset Boulevard), 73 (Jim Young/ Reuters), 114 (Jeff Zelevansky/Icon SMI), 93 (John Zich/zrImages), 11, 57, 59

Getty Images: 123 (Evan Agostini), 76 (Tim Boyle), 113 (CBS Photo Archive), 85 (Timothy A. Clary), 39 (Daniel J. Cox), 27 (Robert Francis), 99 (George Frey), 8 (David McNew), 75 (Panoramic Images), 51 (Edgar Samuel Paxson), 127 (Spencer Platt), 25 bottom (Richard Price), 70 bottom (Chip Somodevilla)

Library of Congress: 58 (Mrs. L. Condon), 61 (Toni Frissell), 52 (William Morris Smith), 54 (Underwood & Underwood), 56, 60

MapQuest.com, Inc.: 69, 131

Minden Pictures: 38 (Carr Clifton), 7 top, 23 (Tim Fitzharris), 36 top (Konrad Wothe)

North Wind Picture Archives/Nancy Carter: 41

Photo Researchers, NY/Chase Studio: 40

PhotoEdit: 125 (Susan Van Etten), 119 top (David Young Wolff), 121 bottom (David Young Wolff)

Reuters/Rick Wilking: 20 bottom

Seapics.com/Mike Johnson: 35

ShutterStock, Inc.: 77, 132 bottom (Heidi Hart), 34 bottom (James Horning), 2, 132 top (Mike Liu), 33 (Sergey I)

Superstock, Inc.: 47 (Jean Leon Gerome Ferris), 72 (Dean Fox)

The Granger Collection, New York: 106 top (Joseph Oriel Eaton), 45 (Charles W. Jefferys), 106 bottom (Frances Benjamin Johnston), 10, 44, 48, 49, 53, 67, 105, 133 bottom

VEER/Digital Vision Photography: cover, 6.

Maps and Illustrations by XNR Productions, Inc.